P9-CFJ-931

EARTH SCIENCES

SECOND EDITION

Ferguson
An imprint of Infobase Publishing

Ferguson
An imprint of Infobase Publishing
132 West 31st Street
New York NY 10001

Library of Congress Cataloging-in-Publication Data

Careers in focus. Earth Science.—2nd ed.
   p. cm.
  Includes bibliographical references and index.
  ISBN-13: 978-0-8160-7272-9
  ISBN-10: 0-8160-7272-8
  1. Earth sciences—Vocational guidance—Juvenile literature. I. J.G. Ferguson Publishing Company. II. Title: Earth science.
  QE34.C37 2008
  550.23—dc22
                                2007038384

Ferguson books are available at special discounts when purchased in bulk quantities for businesses, associations, institutions, or sales promotions. Please call our Special Sales Department in New York at (212) 967-8800 or (800) 322-8755.

You can find Ferguson on the World Wide Web at http://www.fergpubco.com

Text design by David Strelecky
Cover design by TK

Printed in the United States of America

MP MSRF 10 9 8 7 6 5 4 3 2 1

This book is printed on acid-free paper.

Table of Contents

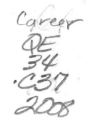

Introduction

Since the earliest time of human history, people have been curious about the world around them. How far does the land go? Why did it rain yesterday but not today? What lives in the ocean? What plants have medicinal value and why? Some of these curious people tried to find answers to such questions by creating stories to explain events, doing experiments that were sometimes dangerous, and going on journeys, perhaps to find the edge of the world. As people developed theories, made discoveries, and built on past knowledge over the centuries, the fields of the earth sciences were born. Today, under the broad category of earth science (also known as geosciences) we include the fields of geography, geology, geophysics, meteorology, and oceanography. Each of these fields, in turn, has its own set of specialties.

Geography forms a bridge between the physical and social sciences. It is concerned with the distribution of people and things and the location of places on the earth's surface, and with the relationships between people and their natural environment. It includes the study of *topography* (the overall arrangement of the land), landforms (mountains, plateaus, plains, and the like), climate, and such features of the natural environment as plants and animals, soils, minerals, and water resources. *Physical geography* is the study of land and water features and the natural forces responsible for their occurrence. This branch includes *climatology* (the study of weather conditions over an extended period of time), *geomorphology,* or *physiography* (the study of surface features and topography), and *mathematical geography* (concerned with the earth's size, shape, and movements). *Human geography* is the study of the way human beings live in their physical and cultural environments. This branch includes *cultural geography* (the study of the geographical distribution of cultural traits), *economic geography* (the study of how people make a living), *political geography* (the study of the influence of geography on nations, national interests, and international relations), *population geography* (the study of the geographical distribution of humans and the analysis of changes in distribution patterns), and *urban geography* (the study of cities and towns in relation to their location, size, shape, and function).

Geology is divided into two main branches. *Physical geology* investigates the composition and structure of rocks and the forces that bring about change in the earth's crust. This branch includes *geochemistry* (the analysis of the chemical composition of the earth's crust), *geomorphology* (the description and study of external forms of the earth's surface), *geophysics* (the application of the principles and techniques of physics to geologic problems of many kinds), *mineralogy* (the study of the chemical and physical properties of minerals), *petrology* (the study of the origin, occurrence, structure, and history of rocks), *seismology* (the study of earthquake shocks and their effects), and *structural geology* (the investigation of stresses and strains in the earth's crust and the deformations they produce). *Historical geology* examines the rocks for evidence of conditions on the earth's surface millions of years ago. It also traces the rise of plant and animal life as revealed by fossils. This branch includes *geochronology* (the study of time in relation to the history of the earth), *paleontology* (the study of fossils), and *stratigraphy* (the classification of rock sequences).

Geophysics, a branch of physical geology, is the application of the science of physics to the study of the earth. Geophysicists have developed highly technical methods for investigating problems in geology, meteorology, and oceanography. Using sensitive instruments, geophysicists measure and describe physical forces that cannot be studied with equal accuracy by direct observation. They are interested primarily in natural forces, such as the forces generated by earthquakes, storms, and ocean currents. Geophysicists help locate oil and mineral deposits, underground water, and the flaws in rock formations at places where roads and dams are to be built.

Meteorology is the science of the atmosphere and its phenomena. It has two major divisions: *weather* refers to the condition of the atmosphere in a specific place at a particular time; *climate* refers to average weather conditions in particular areas over a long period of time.

Oceanography is the science covering all aspects of ocean study and exploration. It draws on the sciences of botany, zoology, meteorology, physics, chemistry, geology, fluid mechanics, and applied mathematics. *Physical oceanography* is the study of water masses and ocean currents, the interaction between the ocean and atmosphere, and the relationship between the sea, weather, and climate. *Chemical oceanography* is the study of the distribution of chemical compounds and chemical interactions that occur in the ocean and the seafloor. *Biological oceanography* is the study of the forms of life in the sea. *Geological* and *geophysical oceanography* is the study of the shape and material of the ocean floor.

The employment outlook for those in earth science positions is generally expected to be good, but variations, of course, may happen among the specialties. Most geologists and geophysicists are employed in the oil and gas industry. Although this industry can be somewhat volatile, the ever-increasing demand for energy resources and the development of new technologies should translate into average employment growth for geologists and geophysicists through 2014. Geologists and geophysicists who have advanced degrees, speak a foreign language, and who are willing to work abroad will have the best employment opportunities. On the domestic front, the prospects for employment may be most favorable in the areas of environmental protection and reclamation. Earth scientists will be needed to help clean up contaminated sites in the United States and help private companies and government agencies comply with environmental regulations.

Positions with agencies dependent on government funding, however, will be closely tied to the status of federal and state budgets. In times of cutbacks, there will be little if any job growth with such agencies.

Most oceanographers' work is research-based, and they will face stiff competition for funding, especially funding from government sources. Opportunities are better for those with advanced education and for those who have expertise in other sciences or engineering.

Overall employment of geographers is expected to grow more slowly than the average through 2014 due to somewhat limited employment opportunities beyond academic and government settings. Businesses, real estate developers, telecommunications companies, and utilities will require geographers to do research and planning. Additionally, geographers who have knowledge of GIS technology as it relates to emergency services, defense, and homeland security applications will have good employment prospects.

Employment for meteorologists is expected to grow about as fast as the average through 2014. The National Weather Service has no plans to increase the number of weather stations or the number of meteorologists in existing stations for many years, and employment of meteorologists in other federal agencies is expected to remain stable. If the health of the economy remains good, however, the outlook in private industry should be better than in the federal sector. Weather-sensitive industries like farming, commodity investments, radio and television, utilities, transportation, and construction firms need more specific weather information than can be provided by the National Weather Service. They will require meteorologists to interpret the results of seasonal and other long-range forecasting research.

Each article in this book discusses in detail a particular occupation in the earth science field. The articles in *Careers in Focus: Earth Science* appear in Ferguson's *Encyclopedia of Careers and Vocational Guidance,* but have been updated and revised with the latest information from the U.S. Department of Labor, professional organizations, and other sources. The following paragraphs detail the sections and features that appear in the book.

The **Quick Facts** section provides a brief summary of the career including recommended school subjects, personal skills, work environment, minimum educational requirements, salary ranges, certification or licensing requirements, and employment outlook. This section also provides acronyms and identification numbers for the following government classification indexes: the *Dictionary of Occupational Titles* (DOT), the *Guide for Occupational Exploration* (GOE), the National Occupational Classification (NOC) Index, and the Occupational Information Network (O*NET)-Standard Occupational Classification System (SOC) index. The DOT, GOE, and O*NET-SOC indexes have been created by the U.S. government; the NOC index is Canada's career classification system. Readers can use the identification numbers listed in the Quick Facts section to access further information about a career. Print editions of the DOT (*Dictionary of Occupational Titles.* Indianapolis, Ind.: JIST Works, 1991) and GOE (*Guide for Occupational Exploration.* Indianapolis, Ind.: JIST Works, 2001) are available at libraries. Electronic versions of the NOC (http://www23.hrdc-drhc.gc.ca) and O*NET-SOC (http://online.onetcenter.org) are available on the Internet. When no DOT, GOE, NOC, or O*NET-SOC numbers are present, this means that the U.S. Department of Labor or Human Resources Development Canada have not created a numerical designation for this career. In this instance, you will see the acronym "N/A," or not available.

The **Overview** section is a brief introductory description of the duties and responsibilities involved in this career. Oftentimes, a career may have a variety of job titles. When this is the case, alternative career titles are presented. Employment statistics are also provided, when available.

The **History** section describes the history of the particular job as it relates to the overall development of its industry or field.

The Job describes the primary and secondary duties of the job.

Requirements discusses high school and postsecondary education and training requirements, any certification or licensing that is necessary, and other personal requirements for success in the job.

Exploring offers suggestions on how to gain experience in or knowledge of the particular job before making a firm educational and financial commitment. The focus is on what can be done while still in high school (or in the early years of college) to gain a better understanding of the job.

The **Employers** section gives an overview of typical places of employment for the job.

Starting Out discusses the best ways to land that first job, be it through the college career services office, newspaper ads, Internet employment sites, or personal contact.

The **Advancement** section describes what kind of career path to expect from the job and how to get there.

Earnings lists salary ranges and describes the typical fringe benefits.

The **Work Environment** section describes the typical surroundings and conditions of employment—whether indoors or outdoors, noisy or quiet, social or independent. Also discussed are typical hours worked, any seasonal fluctuations, and the stresses and strains of the job.

The **Outlook** section summarizes the job in terms of the general economy and industry projections. For the most part, Outlook information is obtained from the U.S. Bureau of Labor Statistics and is supplemented by information gathered from professional associations. Job growth terms follow those used in the *Occupational Outlook Handbook*. Growth described as "much faster than the average" means an increase of 27 percent or more. Growth described as "faster than the average" means an increase of 18 to 26 percent. Growth described as "about as fast as the average" means an increase of 9 to 17 percent. Growth described as "more slowly than the average" means an increase of 0 to 8 percent. "Decline" means a decrease by any amount.

Each article ends with **For More Information,** which lists organizations that provide information on training, education, internships, scholarships, and job placement.

Careers in Focus: Earth Science also includes photographs, informative sidebars, and interviews with professionals in the field.

Botanists

OVERVIEW

Botanists study all different aspects of plant life, from cellular structure to reproduction, to how plants are distributed, to how rainfall or other conditions affect them, and more. Botany is an integral part of modern science and industry, with diverse applications in agriculture, agronomy (soil and crop science), conservation, manufacturing, forestry, horticulture, and other areas. Botanists work for the government, in research and teaching institutions, and for private industry. The primary task of botanists is research and applied research. Nonresearch jobs in testing and inspection, or as lab technicians/technical assistants, also are available. Botany is an extremely diverse field with many specialties.

HISTORY

Plant science is hundreds of years old. The invention of microscopes in the 1600s was very important to the development of modern botany. Microscopes allowed minute study of plant anatomy and cells and led to considerable research in the field. It was in the 1600s that people started using words like *botanographist* or *botanologist*, for one who describes plants.

In the 1700s, Carolus Linnaeus, a Swedish botanist and *taxonomist* (one who identifies, names, and classifies plants) was an important figure. He came up with the two-name (genus and species) system for describing plants that is still used today. In all, Linnaeus wrote more than 180 works on plants, plant diseases, and related subjects.

In Austria during the 19th century monk Gregor Johann Mendel did the first experiments in hybridization. He experimented on garden peas and other plants to figure out why organisms inherit the traits they do. His work is the basis for 20th and 21st century work in plant and animal genetics. As interest in botany grew, botanical gardens became popular in Europe and North America.

Botany is a major branch of biology; the other is zoology. Today, studies in botany reach into many areas of biology, including genetics, biophysics, and other specialized studies. It has taken on particular urgency as a potential source of help for creating new drugs to fight disease, meeting food needs of developing countries, and battling environmental problems.

THE JOB

Research and applied research are the primary tasks of botanists. Literally every aspect of plant life is studied: cell structure, anatomy, heredity, reproduction, and growth; how plants are distributed on the earth; how rainfall, climate, soil, elevation, and other conditions affect plants; and how humans can put plants to better use. In most cases, botanists work at a specific problem or set of problems in their research. For example, they may develop new varieties of crops that will better resist disease. Some botanists focus on a specific type of plant species, such as fungi (mycology), or plants that are native to a specific area, such as a forest or prairie. A botanist working in private industry, for example, for a food or drug company, may focus on the development of new products, testing and inspection, regulatory compliance, or other areas.

Research takes place in laboratories, experiment stations (research sites found at many universities), botanical gardens, and other facilities. Powerful microscopes and special mounting, staining, and preserving techniques may be used in this sort of research.

Some botanists, particularly those working in conservation or ecological areas, also go out into the field. They inventory species, help re-create lost or damaged ecosystems, or direct pollution cleanup efforts.

Nonresearch jobs in testing and inspection or as lab technicians/technical assistants for universities, museums, government agencies, parks, manufacturing companies, botanical gardens, and other facilities also are available.

Botany is an extremely diverse field with many specialties. *Ethnobotanists* study the use of plant life by a particular culture, people,

A botanist gathers samples during a field experiment. *(Peggy Greb/ Agricultural Research Service/U.S. Department of Agriculture)*

or ethnic group to find medicinal uses of certain plants. Study of traditional Native American medicinal uses of plants is an example.

Forest ecologists focus on forest species and their habitats, such as forest wetlands. Related studies include forest genetics and forest economics. Jobs in forestry include work in managing, maintaining, and improving forest species and environments.

Mycologists study fungi and apply their findings in agriculture, medicine, and industry for development of drugs, medicines, molds, and yeasts. They may specialize in research and development in a field such as antibiotics.

Toxicologists study the effect of toxic substances on organisms, including plants. Results of their work may be used in regulatory action, product labeling, and other areas.

Other botanical specialists include *morphologists,* who study macroscopic plant forms and life cycles; *palyologists,* who study pollen and spores; *pteridologists,* who study ferns and other related plants; *bryologists,* who study mosses and similar plants; and *lichenologists,* who study lichens, which are dual organisms made of both alga and fungus.

REQUIREMENTS

High School

To prepare for a career in botany, high school students can explore their interests by taking biology, doing science projects involving plants, and working during summers or school holidays for a nursery, park, or similar operation. College prep courses in chemistry, physics, biology, mathematics, English, and foreign language are a good idea because educational requirements for professional botanists are high. Nonresearch jobs (test and inspection professionals, lab technicians, technical assistants) require at least a bachelor's degree in a biological science or botany; research and teaching positions usually require at least a master's degree or even a doctorate.

Postsecondary Training

At the undergraduate level, there are numerous programs for degrees in botany or biology (which includes studies in both botany and zoology). The master's level and above usually involves a specialized degree. One newer degree is conservation biology, which focuses on the conservation of specific plant and animal communities. The University of Wisconsin–Madison (http://www.nelson.wisc.edu/grad/cbsd) has one of the biggest programs in the United States. Another key school is Yale University's School of Forestry and Environmental Studies (http://environment.yale.edu), which offers degrees in areas such as natural resource management.

Other Requirements

Botanists choose their profession because of their love for plants, gardening, and nature. They need patience, an exploring spirit, the ability to work well alone or with other people, good writing and other communication skills, and tenacity.

EXPLORING

The Botanical Society of America (BSA) suggests that high school students take part in science fairs and clubs and get summer jobs with parks, nurseries, farms, experiment stations, labs, camps, florists, or landscape architects. Hobbies like camping, photography, and computers are useful, too, says the BSA. Tour a botanical garden in your area and talk to staff. You can also get information by contacting national associations. For example, visit the Botanical Society of America's Web site (http://www.botany.org) to read a brochure on careers in botany.

EMPLOYERS

Botanists find employment in the government, in research and teaching institutions, and in private industry. Local, state, and federal agencies, including the Department of Agriculture, Environmental Protection Agency, Public Health Service, Biological Resources Discipline, and the National Aeronautics and Space Administration employ botanists. Countless colleges and universities have botany departments and conduct botanical research. In private industry, botanists work for agribusiness, biotechnology, biological supply, chemical, environmental, food, lumber and paper, pharmaceutical, and petrochemical companies. Botanists also work for greenhouses, arboretums, herbariums, seed and nursery companies, and fruit growers.

STARTING OUT

With a bachelor's degree, a botanist's first job may be as a technical assistant or technician for a lab. Those with a master's degree might get work on a university research project. Someone with a doctorate might get into research and development with a drug, pharmaceutical, or other manufacturer.

For some positions, contract work might be necessary before the botanist gains a full-time position. Contract work is work done on a per-project, or freelance, basis: You sign on for that one project, and then you move on. Conservation groups like The Nature Conservancy (TNC) hire hundreds of contract workers, including ecologists and botanists, each year to do certain work. Contract workers are especially in demand in the summer when there's a lot of biology inventory work to be done.

Opportunities for internships are available with local chapters of TNC. It's also possible to volunteer. Contact the Student Conservation Association for volunteer opportunities. (Contact information can be found at the end of this article.) Land trusts are also good places to check for volunteer work.

ADVANCEMENT

Federal employees generally move up the ranks after gaining a certain number of hours of experience and obtaining advanced degrees. The Botanical Society of America, whose membership primarily comes from universities, notes that key steps for advancing in university positions include producing quality research, publishing research findings in academic and professional journals, and obtaining advanced degrees. Advancing in the private sector depends on the individual employer. Whatever the botanist can do to contribute to the bottom line, such as making breakthroughs in new product development, improving growing methods, and creating better test and inspection methods, will probably help the botanist advance in the company.

EARNINGS

The U.S. Department of Labor reports that biological scientists had median annual salaries of $63,670 in 2005. According to the National Association of Colleges and Employers, in 2005 graduates with a bachelor's degree in biological sciences received average starting salary offers of $31,258 a year; those with master's degrees received offers of $33,600, and those with Ph.D.'s received offers of $42,244. Botanists working for the federal government earned average salaries of $62,207 a year in 2005. Botanists who have advanced training and experience can earn more than $90,000 annually. Benefits vary but usually include paid holidays and vacations, and health insurance.

WORK ENVIRONMENT

Botanists work in a wide variety of settings, some of them very pleasant: greenhouses, botanical gardens, and herbariums, for example. A botanist working for an environmental consultant or conservation organization may spend a lot of time outdoors, rain or shine.

Some botanists interact with the public, such as in a public park or greenhouse, sharing their enthusiasm for the field. Other botanists spend their days in a lab, poring over specimens and writing up the results of their research.

As scientists, botanists need to be focused, patient, and determined. A botanist needs to believe in what he or she is doing and keep at a project until it's completed satisfactorily. The ability to work on one's own is important, but few scientists work in a vacuum. They cooperate with others, share the results of their work orally and in writing, and, particularly in private industry, may need to explain what they're doing in layman's terms.

Some research spans many hours and even years of work. At times, research botanists deeply involved with a project put in a lot of overtime. In exchange, they may be able to work fewer hours other weeks, depending on the specific employer. Botanists performing fieldwork also might have some flexibility of hours. In private industry, the workweek is likely to be a standard 35 to 40 hours.

Educational requirements for botanists are high and so much of the work involves research. Therefore it is important to be a good scholar and enjoy digging for answers.

OUTLOOK

Employment for all biological scientists, including botanists, is expected to grow about as fast as the average for all occupations through 2014, according to the U.S. Department of Labor. Botanists will be needed to help meet growing environmental, conservation, pharmaceutical, and similar demands. However, budget cuts and a large number of graduates have made competition for jobs strong. Government employment opportunities should stay strong, but will depend in part on the continued health of the national economy. Federal budget cuts may jeopardize some projects and positions. Experts say the outlook is best for those with an advanced degree.

FOR MORE INFORMATION

For the booklets Careers in Botany *and* Botany for the Next Millennium, *contact*
Botanical Society of America
PO Box 299
St. Louis, MO 63166-0299

Tel: 314-577-9566
Email: bsa-manager@botany.org
http://www.botany.org

For information on school and internship programs, news on endangered species, and membership information, contact
National Wildlife Federation
11100 Wildlife Center Drive
Reston, VA 20190-5362
Tel: 800-822-9919
http://www.nwf.org

For information about internships with state chapters or at TNC headquarters, contact
The Nature Conservancy (TNC)
4245 North Fairfax Drive, Suite 100
Arlington, VA 22203-1606
Tel: 800-628-6860
Email: comment@tnc.org
http://www.nature.org

To learn about volunteer positions in natural resource management, contact
Student Conservation Association
689 River Road
PO Box 550
Charlestown, NH 03603-0550
Tel: 603-543-1700
http://www.thesca.org

This government agency manages more than 535 national wildlife refuges. The service's Web site has information on volunteer opportunities, careers, and answers to many frequently asked questions.
U.S. Fish & Wildlife Service
U.S. Department of the Interior
1849 C Street, NW
Washington, DC 20240-0001
Tel: 800-344-9453
http://www.fws.gov

Cartographers

OVERVIEW

Cartographers prepare maps, charts, and drawings from aerial photographs and survey data. They also conduct map research, developing new mapping techniques and investigating topics such as how people use maps. Approximately 11,000 cartographers and photogrammetrists are employed in the United States.

HISTORY

Explorers, warriors, and traders have all used maps as a way of navigating around the world or establishing property rights. Early civilizations, such as the Egyptians and the Greeks, used maps drawn on papyrus to show a specific trade route or to trace the conquests of an army. Advances such as the establishment of a system of measuring longitude and latitude helped create more uniform and accurate mapping procedures.

In the 15th and 16th centuries, mapmaking, or cartography, began to change because of the impact of world travel. Explorers such as Christopher Columbus observed and collected geographic information from around the world, which cartographers used to make maps.

Mapmaking continued to develop as surveying and other means of mathematical measurements evolved. Today, the most sophisticated technology is used in compiling geographic information and planning and drafting maps. Such advances have significantly changed the cartographer's job. Computer and satellite technology have been applied to mapmaking with great success. For example, video signals from a satellite detector are digitized and transmitted to earth, where a computer process is used to read the data and create a map with enhanced geographic patterns that can show variations in types of vegetation or soils as well as spatial relationships. With the addition of computer-mapping software and data-merging software, mapping exercises can be done in a fraction of the time that it once took.

THE JOB

Cartographers use manual and computerized drafting instruments, standard mathematical formulas, photogrammetric techniques, and precision stereoplotting apparatuses throughout the mapmaking process. They work with other mapping scientists to plan and draft maps and charts. For example, cartographers may work with land surveyors to interpret geographic information and transfer that information into a series of symbols that are plotted onto a map. They must also be able to plot the names and exact locations of places onto overlays from which a final map is made. Cartographers often work with old maps, using updated information to keep the maps current. Research may also be a part of their job.

Several specializations exist within the field of cartography. *Cartography supervisors* design maps and coordinate and oversee the activities of all those involved in the mapmaking process. Supervisors are most often employed in larger mapmaking operations.

Mosaicists lay out photographic prints on tables, according to the sequence in which the photographs were taken, to form a visual composite of the geographic area. These mosaics are subsequently used in photogrammetric activities such as topographic mapping.

Mean Annual Earnings by Industry, 2005

Federal government	$71,360
Scientific research and development services	$61,420
Power generation and supply	$50,590
Local government	$50,240
Architectural and engineering services	$50,190
Computer systems design and related services	$48,920
State government	$46,230

Source: U.S. Department of Labor

Mosaicists examine aerial photographs in order to verify the location of established landmarks.

Stereoplotter operators also prepare maps from aerial photographs, using instruments that produce simultaneous projections of two photographs taken of the same area.

New technology has made cartography work much more accurate and efficient. Cartographers now use geographic information systems (GIS), which is a computer system that can store, manipulate, and display geographically referenced information. Data is organized by location, stored in map form, and analyzed as a map rather than as a list of numbers. Cartographers use another advanced technology called Global Positioning Systems (GPS) to gather the spatial data used by GIS.

REQUIREMENTS

High School

To prepare for a career in cartography, high school students should study mathematics, geography, mechanical drawing, and computer science. English classes will help hone research and communication skills that students will need to pursue this career. Foreign languages may be helpful in working on maps of other countries.

Postsecondary Training

Mapmaking companies and government agencies prefer that their cartographers hold at least a bachelor's degree. Frequently cartographers have degrees in geography, civil engineering, forestry, or another branch of the physical sciences. In addition, some cartographers have master's degrees in fields such as geography, cartography, and civil engineering.

Other Requirements

Attention to detail is an obvious personal requirement for those working in the field of cartography. Patience and painstaking effort are further requirements. In addition, cartographers should be adept at visualizing objects and distances. These professionals should also be comfortable with computers and with learning new software programs.

EXPLORING

One of the best opportunities for experience is a summer job or internship with a construction firm or other company that prepares maps. The federal government also may have some part-time opportunities for cartographic assistants. While in high school, you can get accustomed to map reading, perhaps through a scouting organization.

EMPLOYERS

There are approximately 11,000 cartographers and photogrammetrists working in the United States. Mapmaking companies are, of course, the primary employers of cartographers. Government agencies, at the federal and the state level, also employ cartographers, as does the military, which has a need for highly specialized maps.

STARTING OUT

Most cartographers are hired upon completion of a bachelor's degree in engineering or geography. A person who is interested in becoming a cartographic technician instead of a full-fledged cartographer may be able to secure an entry-level position after completing a specialized training program. A prospective employer may request a portfolio of completed maps during the interviewing process.

ADVANCEMENT

A cartographer who proves adept at drafting and designing maps and understands the other steps in mapmaking stands a good chance of becoming a supervisor. However, cartographers should expect to work directly on maps throughout their careers, even when holding supervisory positions.

EARNINGS

According to the U.S. Department of Labor, the median yearly income for cartographers and photogrammetrists was $48,250 in 2005. The lowest paid 10 percent of this group earned less than $29,620 during that same time. The highest paid 10 percent, on the other hand, earned more than $79,930. The Cartography and Geographic Information Society reports that cartographers employed by the federal government typically have starting salaries that range from the GS-5 to GS-11 pay levels, depending on such factors as education and experience. In 2007, the GS-5 salary started at $25,623, and the GS-11 salary started at $46,974.

WORK ENVIRONMENT

Cartographers work in office settings with drafting tables and computer-mapping systems. Most cartographers never visit the locations that they are mapping. The average workweek is 35 to 40 hours, although longer hours are occasionally required if a mapping project is on a deadline.

Many cartographers are freelancers who are hired by companies for a specific project. For large map-producing companies, project cartographers may be brought in to help during heavy deadline work. Because of the cost of mapping, most small companies buy rights to maps produced by large firms.

OUTLOOK

Through 2014, employment for cartographers and other mapping scientists is expected to grow about as fast as the average for all occupations. Opportunities will be best for those with excellent technical skills who are able to work with increasingly sophisticated technologies such as GIS and GPS.

FOR MORE INFORMATION

For information on scholarships and colleges and universities offering surveying/geomorphics programs, contact

American Congress on Surveying and Mapping
Six Montgomery Village Avenue, Suite 403
Gaithersburg, MD 20879-3546
Tel: 240-632-9716
Email: dawn.james@acsm.net
http://www.acsm.net

For information on photogrammetry and careers in the field, contact

American Society for Photogrammetry and Remote Sensing
5410 Grosvenor Lane, Suite 210
Bethesda, MD 20814-2160
Tel: 301-493-0290
Email: asprs@asprs.org
http://www.asprs.org

The Cartography and Geographic Information Society is a member organization of the American Congress on Surveying and

Mapping. For membership information and the booklet Cartography and GIS, *contact*

Cartography and Geographic Information Society
Six Montgomery Village Avenue, Suite 403
Gaithersburg, MD 20879-3546
Tel: 240-632-9716
http://www.cartogis.org

For information on cartography, contact

North American Cartographic Information Society
AGS Library
PO Box 399
Milwaukee, WI 53201-0399
Tel: 414-229-6282
http://www.nacis.org

Ecologists

OVERVIEW

Ecology is the study of the interconnections between organisms (plants, animals) and the physical environment. It links biology, which includes both zoology (the study of animals) and botany (the study of plants), with physical sciences such as geology and paleontology. Thus, *ecologist* is a broad name for any of a number of different biological or physical scientists concerned with the study of plants or animals within their environment.

HISTORY

Much of the science that ecologists use is not new. The ancient Greeks recorded their observations of natural history many centuries ago. However, linking together the studies of life and the physical environment is fairly new. Ernst von Haeckel, a German biologist, first defined the term *ecology* in 1866. Like many scientists of his time, he grappled with Charles Darwin's theory of evolution based on natural selection. This theory said that those species of plants and animals that were best adapted to their environment would survive. Although Haeckel did not agree with Darwin, he and many other scientists grew fascinated with the links between living things and their physical environment. At that time, very important discoveries in geology proved that many forms of plants and animals had once existed but had died out. Fossils showed startlingly unfamiliar plant types, for example, as well as prehistoric animal remains that no one had ever imagined existed. (Before such discoveries, people assumed that the species they saw all around them had always existed.) Realization that there were important connections between living things and

An ecologist tests an emperor goose for avian flu. *(Donna Dewhurst/ U.S. Fish & Wildlife Service)*

their physical environment was a key step in the development of the science of ecology.

Like most of the other environmental careers, the professional field of ecology did not really grow popular until the late 1960s and early 1970s. Before then, some scientists and others had tried to warn the public about the ill effects of industrialization, unchecked natural resource consumption, overpopulation, spoiling of wilderness areas, and other thoughtless misuse of the environment. But not until the years after World War II (with growing use of radiation and of pesticides and other chemicals, soaring industrial and automobile pollution, and increasing discharge into waterways) did widespread public alarm about the environment grow. By this time, many feared it was too late. Heavy municipal and industrial discharge into Lake Erie, for example, made it unable to sustain life as before.

In response, the U.S. government passed a series of hard-hitting environmental laws during the 1960s and 1970s. To become compliant with these laws, companies and municipalities began to seek professionals who understood the problems and could help take steps to remedy them. Originally they drew professionals from many existing fields, such as geologists, sanitary engineers, biologists, and chemists. These professionals may not have studied environmental problems as such at school, but they were able to apply the science they knew to the problems at hand.

To some extent, this continues to be true today. Many people working on environmental problems still come from general science or engineering backgrounds. Recently, however, there has been a trend toward specialization. Students in fields such as biology, chemistry, engineering, law, urban planning, and communications can obtain degrees with specialization in the environment. An ecologist today can either have a background in traditional biological or physical sciences or have studied these subjects specifically in the context of environmental problems.

THE JOB

The main area of study in ecology is the ecosystem. Ecosystems are communities of plants and animals within a given habitat that provide the necessary means of survival, including food and water. Ecosystems are defined by such physical conditions as climate, altitude, latitude, and soil and water characteristics. Examples include forests, tundra, savannas (grasslands), and rainforests.

There are many complex and delicate interrelationships within an ecosystem. For example, green plants use the energy of sunlight to make carbohydrates, fats, and proteins; some animals eat these plants and acquire part of the energy of the carbohydrates, fats, and proteins; other animals eat these animals and acquire a smaller part of that energy. Cycles of photosynthesis, respiration, and nitrogen fixation continuously recycle the chemicals of life needed to support the ecosystem. Anything that disrupts these cycles, such as droughts, or the pollution of air or water, can disrupt the delicate workings of the entire ecosystem.

Therefore a primary concern of ecologists today is to study and attempt to find solutions for disruptions in various ecosystems. Increasingly an area of expertise is the reconstruction of ecosystems—that is, the restoration of ecosystems that are destroyed or almost completely destroyed because of pollution, overuse of land, or other action.

According to the Environmental Careers Organization, a key area of work for ecologists is in land and water conservation. They help to restore damaged land and water as well as to preserve wild areas for the future. Understanding the connection between organisms and their physical environments can be invaluable in such efforts.

As an example of how this connection works, imagine that there is a large pond at the edge of a town. A woman out jogging one day notices that hundreds of small, dead fish have washed up at the edge of the pond; a "fish kill," in environmental language. Clearly something is wrong, but what? A nearby factory discharges its wastewater into the pond. Is there something new in the wastewater that killed the fish? Or did something else kill the fish? A professional who understands the fish, the habitat (the pond), the possible reasons for the fish kill, and the potential solutions clearly would be useful here.

This is also true for environmental planning and resource management. Planning involves studying and reporting the impact of an action on the environment. For example, how might the construction of a new federal highway affect the surrounding ecosystem? A planning team may go to the site to view the physical geography and environment, the plants, and the animals. It also may recommend alternative actions that will have less damaging effects.

Resource management means determining what resources already exist and working to use them wisely. Professionals may build databases cataloging the plants, animals, and physical characteristics of a given area. They also may report on what can be done to ensure that the ecosystem can continue to sustain itself in the future. If an ecosystem has been completely destroyed, ecologists can help reconstruct it, getting the physical environment back up to par and reintroducing the species that used to live there.

Ecologists work in many areas of specialization. *Limnologists* study freshwater ecology; *hydrogeologists* focus on water on or below the surface of the earth; *paleontologists* study the remains of ancient life-forms in the form of fossils; *geomorphologists* study the origin of landforms and their changes; and *geochemists* study the chemistry of the earth, including the effect of pollution on the earth's chemistry. Other specialties include *endangered species biologist* and *wetlands ecologist.*

REQUIREMENTS

High School
If you are interested in becoming an ecologist, you should take a college preparatory curriculum while in high school. Classes that will be of particular benefit include earth science, biology, chemistry, English, and math. Because computers are so often involved in various aspects of research and documentation, you should also take computer science courses.

Postsecondary Training
A bachelor of science degree is the minimum degree required for nonresearch jobs, which include testing and inspection. A master's degree is necessary for jobs in applied research or management. A Ph.D. generally is required to advance in the field, including into administrative positions.

The Environmental Careers Organization suggests that if you can only take one undergraduate major, it should be in the basic sciences: biology, botany, zoology, chemistry, physics, or geology. At the master's degree level, natural resource management, ecology, botany, conservation biology, and forestry studies are useful.

Certification or Licensing
The Ecological Society of America offers professional certification at three levels: associate ecologist, ecologist, and senior ecologist. A candidate's certification level will depend on the amount of education and professional experience he or she has. The society encourages certification as a way to enhance ecologists' professional standing in society.

Other Requirements
Ecologists should appreciate and respect nature, and they must also be well versed in scientific fundamentals. Ecologists frequently, but not always, are naturally idealistic. They should be able to work with other people on a team and to express their special knowledge to the other people on the team, who may have different areas of specialization.

EXPLORING

You can seek more information about ecology from guidance counselors and professional ecologists who work at nearby colleges, universities, and government agencies. An easy way to learn more about ecology is to study your own environment. Trips to a nearby pond, forest, or park over the course of several months will provide opportunities to observe and collect data. Science teachers and local park service or arboretum personnel can also offer you guidance.

EMPLOYERS

By far the majority of land and water conservation jobs (about 75 percent) are in the public sector, according to the Environmental Careers Organization. This includes the federal government, which is the largest employer. The Bureau of Land Management, the U.S. Fish and Wildlife Service, the National Park Service, and the U.S. Geological Survey are among the federal agencies that manage U.S. conservation. Other public sector opportunities are with states, regions, and towns. Opportunities in the private sector can be found with utilities, timber companies, and consulting firms. An additional area of employment is in teaching.

STARTING OUT

Internships provide an excellent point of entry into this field. You can volunteer with such groups as the Student Conservation Association (SCA), which places people in resource management projects. Programs include three- to five-week summer internships for high school students. If you have already graduated from high school (and are over age 18), you can check with the SCA for internships in forest, wildlife, resource, and other discipline areas.

Another option is to contact a federal or local government agency directly about an internship. Many, including the Environmental Protection Agency, National Park Service, and Bureau of Land Management, have internship programs. Programs are more informal at the local level.

As for the private sector, an internship with a nonprofit organization may be possible. Such groups include the National Wildlife Federation and the Natural Resources Defense Council.

Entry-level ecologists also may take advantage of temporary or seasonal jobs to gain experience and establish crucial contacts in the field.

ADVANCEMENT

Mid-level biological scientists may move to managerial positions within biology or to nontechnical administrative, sales, or managerial jobs. Ecologists with a Ph.D. may conduct independent research, advance into administrative positions, or teach at the college level, advancing from assistant professor to associate and tenured professorships.

EARNINGS

Salaries for ecologists vary depending on such factors as their level of education, experience, area of specialization, and the organization for which they work. The U.S. Department of Labor reported the median annual income of environmental scientists and specialists was $52,630 in 2005. Salaries ranged from less than $32,910 to $89,040 or more annually. Ecologists working for the federal government in 2005 earned average salaries of $76,160.

Federal agency jobs tend to pay more than state or local agency jobs. Private sector jobs tend to pay more than public sector jobs.

WORK ENVIRONMENT

Ecologists work in a variety of places, from wilderness areas to forests to mountain streams. Ecologists also might work in sewage treatment plants, spend their days in front of computers or in research laboratories, or find themselves testifying in court. A certain amount of idealism probably is useful, though not required. It takes more than just loving nature to be in this field; a person has to be good at scientific fundamentals. Ecologists might start out in the field collecting samples, making notes about animal habits, or doing other monitoring. They may need to be able to work as part of a team and express what they know in terms that everyone on the team can understand.

OUTLOOK

Environmentally oriented jobs are expected to increase about as fast as the average for all occupations through 2014, according to the U.S. Department of Labor. Land and resource conservation jobs tend to be the most scarce, however, because of high popularity and tight budgets for such agencies. Those with advanced degrees will fare better than ecologists with only bachelor's degrees.

FOR MORE INFORMATION

For information on careers in the geosciences, contact
American Geological Institute
4220 King Street
Alexandria, VA 22302-1502
Tel: 703-379-2480
http://www.agiweb.org

In addition to certification, ESA offers a wide variety of publications, including Issues in Ecology, Careers in Ecology, *and fact sheets about specific ecological concerns. For more information, contact*
Ecological Society of America (ESA)
1707 H Street, NW, Suite 400
Washington, DC 20006-3915
Tel: 202-833-8773
Email: esahq@esa.org
http://esa.org

For information on paid internships and careers in the field, contact
Environmental Careers Organization
30 Winter Street, 6th Floor
Boston, MA 02108-4720
Tel: 617-426-4783
http://www.eco.org

For information on internships, job opportunities, and student chapters, contact
National Wildlife Federation
11100 Wildlife Center Drive
Reston, VA 20190-5362
Tel: 800-822-9919
http://www.nwf.org

For information on student volunteer activities and programs, contact
Student Conservation Association
689 River Road
PO Box 550
Charlestown, NH 03603-0550
Tel: 603-543-1700
http://www.thesca.org

INTERVIEW

Dr. Margaret Lowman is the director of environmental initiatives and professor of biology and environmental studies at the New College of Florida. She specializes in forest canopy biology and has traveled throughout the world (including Australia, Peru, Africa, the Americas, and the South Pacific) to pursue her research. (You can learn more about her fascinating career at http://www. canopymeg.com.) Dr. Lowman discussed her career and her work at the New College with the editors of Careers in Focus: Earth Science.

Q. Why did you decide to become a biologist and specialize in the field of forest canopy biology?

A. I wanted to study nature ever since I was about three years old. My best friend, Betsy Hilfiger, and I had tree forts when we were little, and used to nurse birds that had fallen from their nests. We even rescued earthworms that had been cut in half by our dads' lawnmowers and attempted to Band-Aid them back together. Our enthusiasm for the natural world knew no bounds. (Meanwhile, Betsy's brother, Tommy Hilfiger, was in their basement sewing bellbottom jeans, and we thought he was very weird!) I only chose canopy biology when I started my Ph.D. in Australian rain forests, and suddenly realized that most of the forest was much higher than any human could easily reach.

Q. What do you like most and least about your job?

A. I love my job because I believe in conserving the natural world both for the next generation and also because of the importance of ecosystem services, without which we could not survive on this planet. For example, forests provide us with oxygen, with nutrient cycling, and with potential medicines from the chemicals produced by plants. Another example of ecosystem services is the purification of water by streams in the Catskill Mountains, providing good drinking water for New York City at a fraction of the cost of artificial treatment plants. If we leave ecosystems alone, they provide valuable ecosystem services. It makes good economic—as well as ecological—sense to conserve our natural resources, but we need to understand their machinery to take good care of them.

What I like least about my job is that I do not have enough time (or assistants) during the working day to get everything done well. I wish that I had a large grant without strings that would enable me to have a small cadre of helpers to make my ambitious list of conservation projects get done more efficiently!

Q. What advice would you give to high school students who are interested in this career?

A. Students interested in conservation or ecology should try very hard to spend time outdoors, observing nature and learning the inner workings of ecosystems. It is detective work—to hear bird songs, to count biodiversity, and to assess the health of ecosystems. It is very important to experience nature first-hand, not just via computer screens.

Q. Tell us about your work at the New College and the educational opportunities it provides for environmental majors.

A. New College is the liberal arts, honors college for the state of Florida. It has low tuition but quality education. Our environmental science department is small, but we are growing and hoping to offer high-quality training for students to study subtropical ecosystems (Florida's climate is quite similar to that of the tropics). We are planning a biological field station, which will greatly enhance our ability to train students in field ecology—I am busy fund-raising for this project right now!

Q. What advice would you offer environmental majors as they graduate and look for jobs?

A. My advice for students keen to work in the environment: spend time outdoors, always try to take family vacations that visit nature and ecotourism, read and study ecology books, and focus on learning about the lives of other ecologists (you might enjoy reading about my adventures in *Life in the Treetops* or *It's a Jungle Up There*, two books from Yale University Press), and keep your passion for the natural world throughout your working life.

Geographers

OVERVIEW

Geographers study the distribution of physical and cultural phenomena on local, regional, continental, and global scales. There are fewer than 1,000 geographers employed in the United States.

HISTORY

The study of geography developed as people tried to understand their world and answer questions about the size, shape, and scope of the earth.

The ancient Greeks made many contributions to early geography. Aristotle denied the widely held belief that the earth was flat and suggested that it had a spherical shape. Later, the Greek mathematician Eratosthenes calculated the circumference of the earth with remarkable accuracy and developed the concepts of latitude and longitude. The Chinese, Egyptians, Arabs, Romans, and others also made early advances in geography.

Most geographic ideas of the ancient world, including that of the spherical shape of the earth, were lost by Europeans during the Middle Ages. Marco Polo's accounts of his travels in the late 1200s revived interest in geography. Explorations during and after the late 1400s, such as those of Dias, Columbus, da Gama, and Magellan, proved the earth was round and ushered in an age of great discoveries. With it came improved maps and knowledge of the world never before attainable. One of the great mapmakers of the time was Gerhardus Mercator, a 16th-century Flemish geographer.

Richard Hakluyt, an Englishman, and Bernhard Varen, a Dutchman, were notable geographers in the 16th and 17th centuries. The

18th-century German philosopher Immanuel Kant was one of the first persons to write on the subject matter of geography. Geographers of the 19th century included Alexander von Humboldt, Karl Ritter, Friedrich Ratzel, and Albrecht Penck in Germany; Jean Burnhes and Vidal de la Blache in France; Sir Halford Mackinder in Scotland; and William M. Davis in the United States.

Through the years, geography has come to include the study of the earth's surface (that is, the character and structure of an area, including its plant and animal life), as well as the study of economic, political, and cultural life. Thus, the field of geography is concerned with both the physical environment and cultural activities. Some geographers study all these aspects of the earth as they apply to specific regions. More often, however, modern geographers are specialists in one or more subfields of the discipline. These specialists focus on understanding the specific patterns and processes in the physical or human landscape, such as the economic system or the health care delivery system.

THE JOB

Geography can be divided into two broad categories: physical geography and human geography. *Physical geographers* study the processes that create the earth's physical characteristics, such as landforms, soils, vegetation, minerals, water resources, oceans, and weather, and the significance of these processes to humans. *Climatologists* analyze climate patterns and how and why they change. *Geomorphologists,* or *physiographers,* study the origin and development of landforms and interpret their arrangement and distribution over the earth. *Mathematical geographers* study the earth's size, shape, and movements, as well as the effects of the sun, moon, and other heavenly bodies.

Other kinds of physical geographers include *plant geographers, soil geographers,* and *animal geographers.* They study the kinds and distributions of the earth's natural vegetation, soils, and animals. *Cartographers* research data necessary for mapmaking and design and draw the maps. *Computer mappers* are cartographers who use computers and graphics software to draw complex maps.

Human geography is concerned with political organizations, transportation systems, and a wide variety of other cultural activities. *Cultural geographers* study how aspects of geography relate to different cultures. This subspecialty has much in common with archaeology and anthropology.

Regional geographers study all the geographic aspects of a particular area, such as a river basin, an island, a nation, or even an

Learn More About It

Fortey, Richard. *Fossils: The Key to the Past*. 3d ed. Washington, D.C.: Smithsonian Institution Press, 2002.

———. *Life: A Natural History of the First Four Billion Years of Life on Earth*. New York: Random House, 1999.

Marek, Rosanne J. *Opportunities in Social Science Careers*. New York: McGraw-Hill, 2004.

McIvor, Don. *Curiosity's Destinations: Tales & Insights from the Life of a Geologist*. Greenwich, Conn.: Grindstone Press, 2005.

Tarbuck, Edward J., et al. *Applications and Investigations in Earth Science*. 5th ed. Upper Saddle River, N.J.: Prentice Hall, 2005.

Tarbuck, Edward J., and Frederick K. Lutgens. *Earth Science*. Upper Saddle River, N.J.: Prentice Hall, 2005.

Williams, Linda. *Earth Sciences Demystified*. New York: McGraw-Hill, 2004.

entire continent. They are concerned with the physical, economic, political, and cultural characteristics of the area, and they are often called upon to advise on special problems of the region.

Economic geographers analyze the regional distribution of resources and economic activities, including manufacturing, mining, farming, trade, marketing, and communications.

Medical geographers study how health is affected by our physical setting, including environmental quality. They are interested in the way vegetation, minerals in the water supply, climate, and air pollution affect our health. They may also analyze access to health care by geographic region or setting.

Urban geographers, or *urban and regional planners,* focus on metropolitan problems of a geographic nature. They assist in planning and developing urban and suburban projects, such as residential developments, shopping centers, parking areas, and traffic control systems. They also advise business and industry on plant locations and other geographic issues.

Political geographers study such factors as national boundaries and the relation of natural resources and physical features to local, state, national, and international affairs. They also consult and advise on problems of a geopolitical nature.

Geographic information systems (GIS) is a relatively new but rapidly growing field. *Geographic information system specialists* are geographers who combine computer graphics, artificial intelligence, and high-speed communications in the mapping, manipulation, storage, and selective retrieval of geographic data. In this way, they are able to display and analyze a wide variety of natural, cultural, and economic information in applications as diverse as worldwide weather forecasting, emergency management, crime prevention, and the monitoring of metropolitan land use.

REQUIREMENTS

High School
Plan on continuing your education after high school, so take your school's college prep curriculum. Naturally, you will focus on science classes such as geography and earth sciences. In addition, you will benefit from taking classes in sociology, computer science, English, history, and mathematics.

Postsecondary Training
A bachelor's degree with a major in geography is the basic educational requirement for most positions as a professional geographer. Advanced degrees are usually required for most college teaching positions and for those opportunities involving a considerable amount of research activity.

Many colleges and universities offer undergraduate programs in geography. A good number of these institutions also have a curriculum leading to a master's degree or doctorate in geography.

Courses taken by geography students include general physical geography; political, economic, human, urban, and regional geography; and specialized courses such as meteorology and cartography. Undergraduate study usually includes formal classroom instruction, as well as some field study.

Other Requirements
Prospective geographers need basic skills in statistics and mathematics. They should be able to interpret maps and graphs, express ideas in speech and writing, analyze problems, and make sound judgments.

EXPLORING
There are increasing opportunities to gain experience through college internship programs. A few summer and part-time employment opportunities are available in business or industrial firms. Field experiences, offered as part of the college program, provide the

opportunity for potential geographers to test their knowledge and personal qualifications.

You might also want to participate in the National Geography Challenge, which is sponsored by the National Council for Geographic Education. Using a multiple-choice format, you will test your knowledge of geography against students from all over the United States. Ask your geography teacher for more information about the competition.

EMPLOYERS

Fewer than 1,000 geographers are employed in the United States. Many geographers find employment in colleges, universities, and government agencies. Some are employed by business and industrial firms. Most of these positions involve teaching or research responsibilities. A small but growing number of geographers work for map companies, textbook publishers, manufacturers, overseas trading firms, chain stores, market research organizations, real estate developers, environmental consulting firms, travel agencies, banks, and investment firms.

Government agencies that hire geographers include the Central Intelligence Agency, the National Imagery and Mapping Agency, the Bureau of Census, and the U.S. Geological Survey. Some geographers work as business consultants, administrators, or planners.

STARTING OUT

Some beginning jobs are available in teaching geography, mostly in secondary schools. However, high school teaching jobs quite often require study in related fields such as social studies, history, or science. Many beginning geographers find positions connected with mapmaking in either government or private industry. Some obtain positions as research or teaching assistants while working toward advanced degrees. Others enter the planning field. Geographers with advanced degrees can qualify for teaching and research positions at the college level. Many consulting jobs also are available.

Each year the federal government has beginning positions in several geography specialties. Interested students should arrange to take the required civil service examination.

ADVANCEMENT

Advancement is dependent on such factors as amount and type of training, experience, and personal interest and drive. Promotions to jobs requiring more skill and competency are available in all specialty areas. Such jobs are characterized by more administrative, research, or advisory responsibilities in environmental planning.

EARNINGS

Earnings and other benefits depend on the amount of training, the nature of the employment situation, and the personal interests and attributes of the individual employee. According to the U.S. Department of Labor, median annual earnings for geographers were $63,550 in 2005. Salaries ranged from less than $39,040 annually to more than $92,290.

According to the Association of American Geographers, geographers with a bachelor's degree earn between $26,000 and $40,000, while those with a master's degree earn between $35,000 and $50,000. There are positions with community colleges for geographers with master's degrees, while four-year colleges and universities generally require a doctorate. College and university geography professors earned salaries that ranged from less than $34,950 to more than $94,800 in 2005, according to the U.S. Department of Labor. In addition to salaried income, experienced geographers often earn supplemental incomes through consulting, research, and writing activities. Ph.D.'s in industry frequently earn more than those in academia.

WORK ENVIRONMENT

Geographers usually enjoy pleasant working conditions. They spend much of their time in an office or classroom under the typical working conditions of a business, school, or federal agency.

The average workweek of most geographers is 40 hours, particularly for those employed in government or business positions. In some jobs, however, there can be unusual work situations. Fieldwork often requires the geographer to spend an extended period of time living in remote areas, often under primitive conditions.

OUTLOOK

Geography is a very small profession. With the increased emphasis on planning and research in U.S. business and government, however, the number of geographers in business has doubled in recent years. According to the *Occupational Outlook Handbook*, employment opportunities for geographers are expected to grow more slowly than the average for all occupations through 2014. Despite this prediction, the use of GIS technology in traditional and nontraditional settings, such as emergency services, defense, and homeland security, will create many new opportunities for qualified geographers.

Geographers will be needed to analyze or select sites for commercial construction, such as new shopping centers, supermarkets, and industrial parks. There will also be a demand for geographers to work in urban renewal projects, highway programs, real estate development, the telecommunications industry, and environmental planning. Competition for college and university teaching jobs is stiff. Many geographers with graduate degrees seek research and management positions in government and private industry. Others fill nonacademic positions in cartography, health services, climatology, flood management, conservation, and environmental planning.

FOR MORE INFORMATION

For maps, books, journals, and other geography-related materials, contact
American Geographical Society
120 Wall Street, Suite 100
New York, NY 10005-3904
Tel: 212-422-5456
Email: AGS@amergeog.org
http://www.amergeog.org

To order a copy of the publication Careers in Geography, *visit the AAG Web site.*
Association of American Geographers (AAG)
1710 16th Street, NW
Washington, DC 20009-3198
Tel: 202-234-1450
Email: gaia@aag.org
http://www.aag.org

To read Finding a Way Through Career Geography, *visit the council's Web site.*
National Council for Geographic Education
Jacksonville State University
206A Martin Hall
Jacksonville, AL 36265-1602
Tel: 256-782-5293
http://www.ncge.org

For information on opportunities for women in geography, contact
Society of Women Geographers
415 East Capitol Street, SE
Washington, DC 20003-3810
Tel: 202-546-9228
Email: swghq@verizon.net
http://www.iswg.org

Geographic Information Systems Specialists

OVERVIEW

Geographic information systems (GIS) specialists focus on the scientific theory of geographic information and analysis, and may research and develop new geographic information systems and applications. They combine computer graphics, artificial intelligence, and high-speed communications in the mapping, manipulation, storage, and selective retrieval of geographic data.

HISTORY

Geographic information systems (GIS) have grown up along with the rest of the computer industry in the past 25 to 30 years and have been pushed along, particularly in the last 10 years, by aggressive GIS software developers, extensive research and development, and widespread application of GIS in many different professional fields.

GIS is a huge field with applications ranging from health to business to managing utilities to tracking land ownership. For example, using spatial analysis, city officials might map the outbreak of an illness with the GIS helping to determine information like where the majority of cases are occurring and the demographics of the victims, such as their race, educational level, or other data.

Such systems also are a natural for environmental work, including environmental planning and natural resource management. To designate a site for a new recreational area of a specific size, a certain distance from the highway, and on government land, GIS can locate parcels of land owned by the government that match the size requirement, and show boundaries of the highway. By overlaying all the pieces, specialists can determine which site is the best.

THE JOB

GIS is basically a computer system that can assemble, store, manipulate, and display geographically referenced information. GIS specialists use this computer technology to combine mapmaking techniques with massive databases. The data are catalogued according to location, stored in map form, and analyzed as though they were a map rather than a list. The databases might include physical geographic data, demographics, census information, or epidemiology. Environmental planning and natural resource management find GIS particularly useful, but the techniques are now being applied to a variety of disciplines, including scientific investigations, homeland defense, and crime analysis.

Planners and developers develop a detailed scheme for a project before any work is begun to make sure objectives are met, whether they are saving a wildlife habitat, putting a transportation system in place, or guiding a booming city's expansion. Such projects require an environmental impact statement documenting the effect of the project on the environment. GIS quickly integrates lots of different types of data so that planners can spend more of their time studying the data and developing solutions.

GIS can show two- or three-dimensional maps of a region's natural features; current land and water use; distribution of housing, recreational areas, industry, and other existing development; ownership patterns; demographics of current residents; and other information. GIS then might be used to simulate growth patterns for the area and try various development plans to anticipate and prevent adverse environmental impacts.

In natural resource management, research scientists use GIS as part of efforts to build understanding about the natural resources. For example, geologists and other research scientists for the U.S. Geological Survey gather and study data relating to coastal erosion and pollution, such as along the mid-Atlantic coast, Gulf Coast, and other areas, in order to help them learn how to stop the erosion. This data includes everything from the movement of sediment during storms to wind, wave, and weather patterns. Systems that allow the scientists to pull all the data together and analyze it in different ways are indispensable in such work.

GIS specialists are computer experts. *Digitizers* are entry-level GIS workers with little experience. They convert hard-copy maps to digital formats. *GIS technicians* have more experience with GIS software, such as ArcView and ArcInfo, and do mapmaking (cartographic output) and data manipulation. They are able to do some basic computer programming. *GIS analysts* perform more complex analysis and relational database management, and they have more programming experience. Most GIS software is designed to allow specialists to customize it using object-oriented programming languages, such as Visual Basic. *Geographic information officers* are GIS specialists who manage, plan, and develop strategies relating to GIS technology at the institutional level.

REQUIREMENTS

High School

To prepare for this career while in high school, a college preparatory program is recommended. You will need a strong background in science, mathematics, and especially computer science, so take as many of these classes as your school offers. In addition, history classes, which will teach you about different countries and their relationships to each other, will be valuable. English courses will help you develop your research and writing skills. Also, consider taking a foreign language. This may help you fulfill some later college requirements as well as give you exposure to new words and place names and a sense of other cultures.

Postsecondary Training

According to a survey by the Urban and Regional Information Systems Association (URISA) published in 2007, 85 percent of information technology (IT) and GIS professionals hold a bachelor's degree or higher. Degrees were most commonly in geography, GIS, planning, engineering, and computer science. According to the Environmental Systems Research Institute (ESRI), there are more than 200 degree or certificate programs in GIS worldwide.

Most employers require GIS specialists to be at least somewhat proficient with GIS software. According to the URISA survey, the most popular software programs were ESRI's ArcGIS and ArcSDE.

GIS specialists also need skills in report writing, technical support, and teaching/training.

Certification or Licensing

GIS specialists can receive voluntary certification from the GIS Certification Institute. Applicants must have a baccalaureate degree in any field, complete coursework and other documented education in GIS and geospatial data technologies, have work experience in a GIS-related position, and participate in conferences or GIS-related events. Applicants who meet all certification requirements may use the designation certified GIS professional. Certification must be renewed every five years.

Other Requirements

GIS specialists, naturally, must enjoy using computers and keeping up with technology developments that will affect their work, such as new software and new hardware. They should be detail-oriented. Frequently, the projects GIS specialists work on are part of a team effort. These specialists, therefore, should be able to work well with others, meet deadlines, and clearly explain their findings. To keep up with their industry and advance in their jobs, GIS specialists must be committed to lifelong learning.

EXPLORING

Become comfortable with and read up on computers. There are books available on GIS that will give you a good introduction to the field. For example, you might explore ESRI's *GIS for Everyone,* which has an accompanying CD-ROM and Web site (http://www. esri.com/gisforeveryone). Check out the institute's Web site (http:// www.esri.com) for other books and educational tools. Read GIS publications like *GEOWorld* (http://www.geoplace.com), *Spatial- News* (http://spatialnews.geocomm.com), or *Geospatial Solutions* (http://www.geospatial-online.com/geospatialsolutions). Finally, if possible, visit a business that uses GIS and ask questions. You might try contacting a local college or local environmental agency for contact names of users in the area.

EMPLOYERS

According to URISA's 2007 survey of IT/GIS professionals, 63.7 percent of respondents work in some level of government, from local through federal agencies.

GIS most often is used as part of a professional discipline, such as health, engineering, business, or emergency services. Large users of GIS include Lockheed Martin and other government defense contractors, government agencies and municipalities, and medical departments. GIS software developers who sell big GIS software packages need research and development people to create new packages, write manuals, and do other development work; sales and marketing people; and administrative people.

STARTING OUT

Look in GIS trade magazines for job opportunities or check with the career services department of your community college, college, or university. Search the Internet for sites that specialize exclusively in GIS employment opportunities. Those interested in focusing on GIS science most likely will find opportunities with research institutes, colleges, and universities.

ADVANCEMENT

Advancement depends on the specific field and employer. Those working for a GIS company might rise from an analyst or software engineering position to manager, or move over to sales and marketing. Where GIS is applied as part of a professional discipline such as engineering, advanced knowledge of GIS may help a job candidate stand out from the crowd and move ahead in his or her field.

EARNINGS

URISA's *2007 Salary Survey* found that on average, respondents earned $60,050 in 2006. GeoCommunity.com reported the following salary ranges for GIS workers by specialty in 2006: GIS technician, $10,000 to $59,999; GIS analyst, $10,000 to $50,000 or more; GIS programmer, $20,000 to $80,000 or more; GIS coordinator, $20,000 to $60,000 or more; and GIS manager, $30,000 to $70,000 or more.

WORK ENVIRONMENT

Geographic information systems are normally found in typical corporate or office environments. They usually consist of PC-based workstations with big screens. (Some applications also are available for Macs, but the majority are for PCs.) In an organization where GIS is used extensively, each person might have a GIS workstation at his or her desk.

OUTLOOK

The U.S. Department of Labor predicts that employment in the areas of surveying and mapping will grow about as fast as the average for all occupations through 2014. The outlook for GIS specialists in environmental work, emergency services (fire and police rescues), and homeland defense is strong. GIS maps, drawings, animations, and other cartographic images will allow scientists, researchers, and public safety officials to view geographic information in new ways. Variations can be tracked over time and possible future changes can be projected and rendered visually. Environmental planning will be another significant area of growth for GIS technology, and federal and local government agencies will continue to be the primary employers of GIS specialists. Private sector opportunities may see some growth in areas such as health care, real estate, retail marketing, tourism, agriculture, petroleum, and telecommunications.

FOR MORE INFORMATION

For information on careers in the field, contact
American Society for Photogrammetry and Remote Sensing
5410 Grosvenor Lane, Suite 210
Bethesda, MD 20814-2160
Tel: 301-493-0290
Email: asprs@asprs.org
http://www.asprs.org/career

For more information on careers in GIS and geography, visit the AAG Web site.
Association of American Geographers (AAG)
1710 16th Street, NW
Washington, DC 20009-3198
Tel: 202-234-1450
Email: gaia@aag.org
http://www.aag.org

For industry news, software developments, and publications, contact
Environmental Systems Research Institute
380 New York Street
Redlands, CA 92373-8100
Tel: 800-447-9778
http://www.esri.com

For more information on certification, contact
GIS Certification Institute
1460 Renaissance Drive, Suite 305
Park Ridge, IL 60068-1348
Tel: 847-824-7768
Email: sgrams@gisci.org
http://www.gisci.org

For information on colleges and universities offering certificate programs in GIS, contact
Urban and Regional Information Systems Association
1460 Renaissance Drive, Suite 305
Park Ridge, IL 60068-1348
Tel: 847-824-6300
Email: info@urisa.org
http://www.urisa.org

This science agency of the U.S. Department of the Interior has information on geospatial data, publications, education, and more on its Web site.
U.S. Geological Survey
National Center
12201 Sunrise Valley Drive
Reston, VA 20192-0002
Tel: 703-648-4000
http://www.usgs.gov

ESRI has created the site GIS.com, which provides information on topics such as what GIS is, GIS training, and GIS specialties.
GIS.com
http://www.gis.com

Geological Technicians

QUICK FACTS

School Subjects
Earth science
Mathematics

Personal Skills
Helping/teaching
Technical/scientific

Work Environment
Indoors and outdoors
One location with some
travel

Minimum Education Level
High school diploma

Salary Range
$21,630 to $43,750 to
$84,650+

Certification or Licensing
None available

Outlook
More slowly than the average

DOT
024

GOE
02.05.01

NOC
2212

O*NET-SOC
19-4041.00, 19-4041.01,
19-4041.02

OVERVIEW

Geological technicians assist geologists in their studies of the earth's physical makeup and history. This includes the exploration of a wide variety of phenomena, such as mountain uplifting, rock formations, mineral deposition, earthquakes, and volcanic eruptions. Modern geology is particularly concerned with the exploration for mineral and petroleum deposits in the earth and with minimizing the effects of man-made structures on the environment.

Petroleum technicians measure and record the conditions of oil and gas wells. They use instruments lowered into the wells, and evaluate mud from the wells. They examine data to determine petroleum and mineral content.

There are approximately 11,000 geological and petroleum technicians employed in the United States.

HISTORY

Because of our reliance on petroleum and natural gas to help us meet so many of our basic needs, many geologists have focused in recent years on the exploration for new deposits of these fossil fuels. Natural gas provides fuel for ovens and for furnaces to heat homes. Petroleum is refined into gasoline for cars, grease to keep machinery parts operating smoothly, and plastic, tar, and kerosene, among other products.

Small companies and large multinational corporations send teams of geologists and drill operators to scour farms, deserts, and the ocean floor for new deposits of oil. One of the most important members on these teams is the geological technician.

Facts about the Earth

- Scientists believe that the earth is 4.5 to 4.6 million years old.
- The earth has seven continents: Africa, Antarctica, Asia, Australia, Europe, North America, and South America.
- Mt. Everest in Asia is the highest mountain in the world—towering 29,035 feet above sea level.
- The lowest place on earth is the Dead Sea at 1,369 feet below sea level.
- The deepest point in the ocean is Challenger Deep in the Mariana Trench in the Western Pacific Ocean. It is 35,840 feet below sea level.
- The highest temperature ever recorded was a blazing 135.8°F in Al Aziziyah, Libya, on September 13, 1922.
- The lowest temperature ever recorded was a bone-chilling -128.5°F in Vostok, Antarctica, on July 21, 1983.
- Nearly 71 percent of the earth is made up of water.
- Earth's atmosphere is made up of 77 percent nitrogen, 21 percent oxygen, and small amounts of carbon dioxide, argon, and water.

Source: About.com

THE JOB

Geological technicians most often work under the supervision of a geologist or other geoscientist as part of a research team. Areas of specialization include *environmental geology,* the study of how pollution, waste, and hazardous materials affect the earth; *geophysics,* the study of the earth's interior and magnetic, electric, and gravitational fields; *hydrology,* the investigation of the movement and quality of surface water; *petroleum geology*, the exploration and production of crude oil and natural gas; and *seismology,* the study of earthquakes and the forces that cause them.

The most common employment for geological technicians is with *petroleum geologists*. These scientists determine where deposits of oil and natural gas may be buried beneath the earth's surface. Using data gathered from workers in the field, geological technicians draft maps displaying where drilling operations are taking place and create reports that geologists use to determine where an oil deposit might be located.

Geological technicians draft maps that pinpoint the exact location where a drilling crew has dug a well. In addition to indicating whether or not oil was found, the map also specifies the depth of the well. If oil is located, the information on the map enables geologists to determine the probable size of the oil deposit.

Technicians also analyze various types of raw data when creating reports. Crews often, for example, detonate carefully planned explosions that send shock waves deep into the earth. Microphones record these waves. Geologists study the patterns of the waves to determine the composition of rock beneath the surface. Geological technicians take these patterns and remove any background noise, such as sound waves from an airplane passing overhead, and then write a report that summarizes what the sound patterns indicate.

Some geological technicians work in the field of environmental engineering. Assisting geologists, they study how structures, such as roads, landfills, and commercial, residential, and industrial developments, affect the environment. The information they gather is incorporated into environmental impact statements, which are used by developers, government officials, and private landowners to minimize damage to the environment.

REQUIREMENTS

High School

You will need a high school diploma if you are considering a career as a geological technician and hope to advance into supervisory positions. Though some people acquire their skills on the job, it is helpful to begin your preparation in high school.

Courses in geology, geography, and mathematics, including algebra, trigonometry, and statistics, are all recommended. Drafting courses can teach important mapmaking skills, and courses in computer science are useful since many companies now design maps using computer software. Additionally, courses in English and speech will help you develop the communication skills necessary for writing reports and serving as a liaison between geologists and field crews.

Postsecondary Training

Though not required, some postsecondary education may be helpful in finding a job, particularly in the increasingly competitive oil and gas industry. A bachelor of science degree, with an emphasis in geology, advanced mathematics, and drafting, is recommended. Some companies will not hire technicians without a degree. Some two-year colleges offer an associate's degree for geological technicians.

Other Requirements

In addition to academic preparation, successful technicians are detail-oriented and have excellent time management and organizational skills. Drilling for oil, for example, can be a costly and time-consuming venture. Competence in interpreting data is crucial because oil companies and other employers rely heavily on the accuracy of information reported by their geological technicians.

EXPLORING

School counselors and librarians are a good source of information about careers. A science teacher may also be helpful in providing specific information about a career as a geological aide. Large oil and gas companies, such as Chevron, Texaco, and Shell Oil Company, may be able to provide information about careers in the geological sciences, and some of these companies occasionally offer educational programs for high school students and opportunities for summer employment.

In addition to studying geology in school and contacting employers to learn about the profession, you should consider joining a geology-related club or organization, for example, concerned with rock collecting. Local amateur geological groups also offer opportunities to gain exposure to the geological sciences.

EMPLOYERS

Approximately 11,000 geological and petroleum technicians are employed in the United States. Technicians are employed by major oil and gas companies. Environmental consulting and environmental engineering firms may also be a source of employment in the private sector. With these firms, geological technicians assist in creating environmental impact studies.

The federal government hires geologists and may employ geological technicians in the Department of the Interior (specifically in the U.S. Geological Survey and the Bureau of Reclamation) and in the Departments of Defense, Agriculture, and Commerce.

State agencies, nonprofit research organizations, and state-funded museums are also possible sources of employment for geological technicians.

STARTING OUT

After completing high school or college, the prospective geological technician can look for work in various areas, including private industry and government. The exploration departments of oil and gas companies are the first places to look for a position as a geological technician. Most are multinational corporations and are likely to have many geological technicians on staff in the United States, as well as in overseas departments.

Internships and volunteerships should be considered. Large corporations and professional associations are resources for internship information. Volunteer opportunities are also available.

ADVANCEMENT

Advancement for geological technicians depends on the size of the organization they work for and their educational background. At smaller companies and consulting firms, the range of tasks may be quite varied. Geological technicians may perform some tasks that geologists normally do, as well as some clerical duties. At larger companies, the opposite may be true. A geological technician might specialize in well spotting, for example, or supervise a staff of several geological technicians.

Supervisory positions are often available to technicians with several years of on-the-job experience. Typically, these technicians will train new staff in proper procedures and methods, as well as check their work for accuracy before sending it to the geologist.

With additional education and either a master's degree or doctorate, geological technicians can go on to work as geologists, soil scientists, or paleontologists, for example.

EARNINGS

Salaries for geological technicians working in the petroleum and gas industry vary between regions. Within the state of Texas, for example, salaries are typically higher in the Houston area, where more drilling occurs, than in Odessa-Midland, where petroleum and gas exploration have tapered off in recent years.

According to the U.S. Department of Labor, geological and petroleum technicians earned salaries that ranged from less than $21,630 to more than $84,650 in 2005. The average salary for these technicians was $43,750 in 2005.

WORK ENVIRONMENT

Geological technicians frequently work out in the field, where drilling or testing is occurring. In these situations, technicians may spend considerable time outdoors in primitive or rugged conditions. Sometimes this involves camping for several days in a remote location.

Geological technicians who are employed in a laboratory or office generally work regular 40-hour weeks in pleasant conditions. The work each day is fairly routine. It may involve gathering data from the previous day's tests, examining preliminary reports from drilling crews, drafting maps, and writing reports for the geologist.

Geological technicians provide important support to geologists and other geoscientists. They are responsible for the accurate organization and presentation of important data. In a petroleum company, for example, geological technicians are a crucial link in the search to locate hidden pockets of fossil fuel. They shoulder a lot of responsibility for the successful outcome of exploratory drilling operations. While this may at times be stressful, it is also rewarding because geological technicians are able to see tangible results from their work.

OUTLOOK

The U.S. Department of Labor predicts that employment for geological technicians will grow more slowly than the average for all occupations through 2014 due to declines in the oil and gas extraction and mining industries—which employ a large percentage of these workers. Despite this prediction, technicians should have good opportunities—especially in the energy industry—as there is a shortage of qualified job candidates.

Geological technicians who speak a foreign language and who are willing to work abroad should enjoy the best opportunities. In addition, job opportunities in environmental consulting will continue to be good as long as environmental regulations remain intact.

Though geological technicians tend to have training that is best suited to their own field, they might find employment with companies that value their mapmaking and drafting abilities. Public utility companies, architectural firms, developers, and some private consulting firms might have a need for these skills.

FOR MORE INFORMATION

For information on the geophysical sciences, contact
American Geophysical Union
2000 Florida Avenue, NW
Washington, DC 20009-1277
Tel: 800-966-2481
http://www.agu.org

For information on careers in geology, contact the following organizations:
American Geological Institute
4220 King Street
Alexandria, VA 22302-1502
Tel: 703-379-2480
http://www.agiweb.org

Geological Society of America
PO Box 9140
Boulder, CO 80301-9140
Tel: 888-443-4472
Email: gsaservice@geosociety.org
http://www.geosociety.org

For career information and profiles of women in geophysics, visit the AWG's Web site.
Association for Women Geoscientists (AWG)
PO Box 30645
Lincoln, NE 68503-0645
Email: office@awg.org
http://www.awg.org

For career and educational information about the geosciences, visit
U.S. Geological Survey
http://www.usgs.gov/education

Geologists often begin their careers in field exploration or as research assistants in laboratories. As they gain experience, they are given more difficult assignments and may be promoted to supervisory positions, such as project leader or program manager.

ADVANCEMENT

A geologist with a bachelor's degree has little chance of advancing to higher-level positions. Continued formal training and work experience are necessary, especially as competition for these positions grows more intense. A doctorate is essential for most college or university teaching positions and is preferred for much research work.

EARNINGS

Graduates with a bachelor's degree in the geological sciences earned about $39,365 annually in 2005, according to the National Association of Colleges and Employers.

The U.S. Department of Labor reports that the median annual salary for geoscientists was $71,640 in 2005; the top 10 percent earned more than $135,290, while the lowest 10 percent earned less than $39,420 a year. In the federal government, the average salary for geologists in managerial, supervisory, and nonsupervisory positions was $86,110 a year in 2005.

Although the petroleum, mineral, and mining industries offer higher salaries, competition for these jobs is stiff and there is less job security than in other areas. In addition, college and university teachers can earn additional income through research, writing, and consulting. Salaries for foreign assignments may be significantly higher than those in the United States.

WORK ENVIRONMENT

Some geologists spend most of their time in a laboratory or office, working a regular 40-hour week in pleasant conditions; others divide their time between fieldwork and office or laboratory work. Those who work in the field often travel to remote sites by helicopter or four-wheel drive vehicle and cover large areas on foot. They may camp for extended periods of time in primitive conditions with the members of the geological team as their only companions. Exploration geologists often work overseas or in remote areas, and job relocation is not unusual. Marine geologists may spend considerable time at sea.

OUTLOOK

According to the *Occupational Outlook Handbook,* employment of geologists is expected to grow more slowly than the average for all occupations through 2014. Despite this prediction, opportunities in the field are expected to be good because a large number of geologists are expected to retire from the field during the next decade.

Additionally, in response to the curtailed petroleum activity in the 1990s, the number of graduates in geology and geophysics, especially petroleum geology, dropped considerably in the last decade. Relative stability has now returned to the petroleum industry, increasing the need for qualified geoscientists. With improved technology and greater demand for energy resources, job opportunities are expected to be good, especially for those with a master's degree and those familiar with computer modeling and the global positioning system (GPS). Geologists who are able to speak a foreign language and who are willing to work overseas will also have strong employment prospects. In addition to the oil and gas industries, geologists will be able to find jobs in environmental protection and reclamation.

FOR MORE INFORMATION

For information on geoscience careers, contact
American Geological Institute
4220 King Street
Alexandria, VA 22302-1502
Tel: 703-379-2480
http://www.agiweb.org

For information on careers, certification, and scholarships, contact
American Institute of Professional Geologists
1400 West 122nd Avenue, Suite 250
Westminster, CO 80234-3499
Tel: 303-412-6205
Email: aipg@aipg.org
http://www.aipg.org

For career information and profiles of women in geophysics, visit the AWG Web site.
Association for Women Geoscientists (AWG)
PO Box 30645
Lincoln, NE 68503-0645

Geologists

OVERVIEW

Geologists study all aspects of the earth, including its origin, history, composition, and structure. Along more practical lines, geologists may, through the use of theoretical knowledge and research data, locate groundwater, oil, minerals, and other natural resources. They play an increasingly important role in studying, preserving, and cleaning up the environment. They advise construction companies and government agencies on the suitability of locations being considered for buildings, highways, and other structures. They also prepare geological reports, maps, and diagrams. According to the U.S. Department of Labor, there are approximately 28,000 geoscientists employed in the United States, which includes geologists, geophysicists, and oceanographers.

HISTORY

Geology is a young science, first developed by early mining engineers. In the late 18th century, scientists such as A. G. Werner and James Hutton, a retired British physician, created a sensation with their differing theories on the origins of rocks. Through the study of fossils and the development of geological maps, others continued to examine the history of the earth in the 19th century.

From these beginnings, geology has made rapid advances, both in scope and knowledge. With the development of more intricate technology, geologists are able to study areas of the earth they were previously unable to reach. Seismographs, for example, measure energy waves resulting from the earth's movement in order to

QUICK FACTS

School Subjects
Earth science
Geography

Personal Skills
Helping/teaching
Technical/scientific

Work Environment
Indoors and outdoors
One location with some travel

Minimum Education Level
Bachelor's degree

Salary Range
$39,365 to $71,640 to $135,290+

Certification or Licensing
Voluntary (certification)
Required by certain states (licensing)

Outlook
More slowly than the average

DOT
024

GOE
02.02.01

NOC
2113

O*NET-SOC
19-2042.01

determine the location and intensity of earthquakes. Seismic prospecting involves bouncing sound waves off buried rock layers.

THE JOB

The geologist's work includes locating and obtaining physical data and material. This may necessitate the drilling of deep holes to obtain samples, the collection and examination of the materials found on or under the earth's surface, or the use of instruments to measure the earth's gravity and magnetic field. Some geologists may spend three to six months of each year in fieldwork. In laboratory work, geologists carry out studies based on field research. Sometimes working under controlled temperatures or pressures, geologists analyze the chemical and physical properties of geological specimens, such as rock, fossil remains, and soil. Once the data is analyzed and the studies are completed, geologists and geological technicians write reports based on their research.

A wide variety of laboratory instruments are used, including X-ray diffractometers, which determine the crystal structure of minerals, and petrographic microscopes for the study of rock and sediment samples.

Geologists working to protect the environment may design and monitor waste disposal sites, preserve water supplies, and reclaim contaminated land and water to comply with federal environmental regulations.

Geologists often specialize in one of the following disciplines:

Marine geologists study the oceans, including the seabed and subsurface features.

Paleontologists specialize in the study of the earth's rock formations, including fossilized remains of plant and animal life, in order to understand the earth's evolution and estimate its age.

Geochronologists are geoscientists who use radioactive dating and other techniques to estimate the age of rock and other samples from an exploration site.

Petroleum geologists attempt to locate natural gas and oil deposits through exploratory testing and study of the data obtained. They recommend the acquisition of new properties and the retention or release of properties already owned by their companies. They also estimate oil reserves and assist petroleum engineers in determining exact production procedures.

Closely related to petroleum geologists are *economic geologists*, who search for new resources of minerals and fuels.

A geologist works on a road cut. *(Bob Daemmrich/The Image Works)*

Engineering geologists are responsible for the application of geological knowledge to problems arising in the construction of roads, buildings, bridges, dams, and other structures.

Mineralogists are interested in the classification of minerals composing rocks and mineral deposits. To this end, they examine and analyze the physical and chemical properties of minerals and precious stones to develop data and theories on their origin, occurrence, and possible uses in industry and commerce.

Petrologists study the origin and composition of igneous, metamorphic, and sedimentary rocks.

Stratigraphers study the distribution and relative arrangement of sedimentary rock layers. This enables them to understand evolutionary changes in fossils and plants, which leads to an understanding of successive changes in the distribution of land and sea.

Closely related to stratigraphers are *sedimentologists,* who determine processes and products involved in sedimentary rock formations.

Geohydrologists study the nature and distribution of water within the earth and are often involved in environmental impact studies.

Geomorphologists study the form of the earth's surface and the processes that bring about changes, such as erosion and glaciation.

Glacial geologists study the physical properties and movement of ice sheets and glaciers.

The geologist is far from limited in a choice of work, but a basic knowledge of all sciences is essential in each of these specializations. An increasing number of scientists combine geology with detailed knowledge in another field. *Geochemists,* for example, are concerned with the chemical composition of, and the changes in, minerals and rocks, while *planetary geologists* apply their knowledge of geology to interpret surface conditions on other planets and the moon.

REQUIREMENTS

High School

Because you will need a college degree in order to find work in this profession, you should take a college preparatory curriculum while in high school. Such a curriculum will include computer science, history, English, and geography classes. Science and math classes are also important, particularly earth science, chemistry, and physics. Math classes should include algebra, trigonometry, and statistics.

Postsecondary Training

A bachelor's degree is the minimum requirement for entry into lower-level geology jobs, but a master's degree is usually necessary for beginning positions in research, teaching, and exploration. A person with a strong background in physics, chemistry, mathematics, or computer science may also qualify for some geology jobs. For those wishing to make significant advancements in research and in teaching at the college level, a doctoral degree is required. Those interested in the geological profession should have an aptitude not only for geology but also for physics, chemistry, and mathematics.

A number of colleges, universities, and institutions of technology offer degrees in geology. In addition, programs in geophysical technology, geophysical engineering, geophysical prospecting, and engineering geology offer related training for beginning geologists as well.

Traditional geoscience courses emphasize classical geologic methods and concepts. Mineralogy, paleontology, stratigraphy, and structural geology are important courses for undergraduates. Students interested in environmental and regulatory fields should take courses in hydrology, hazardous waste management, environmental legislation, chemistry, fluid mechanics, and geologic logging.

In addition, students should take courses in related sciences, mathematics, English composition, and computer science. Students seeking graduate degrees in geology should concentrate on advanced courses in geology, placing major emphasis on their particular fields.

Certification or Licensing

The American Institute of Professional Geologists (AIPG) grants the certified professional geologist (CPG) designation to geologists who have earned a bachelor's degree or higher in the geological sciences and have eight years of professional experience (applicants with a master's degree need only seven years of professional experience and those with a Ph.D., five years). Candidates must also undergo peer review by three professional geologists (two of whom must be CPGs) and pay an application fee.

The institute also offers the registered member designation to geologists who are registered in various states and are not seeking AIPG certification. Applicants must have at least a bachelor's degree in the geological sciences with at least 30 semester hours of geology, be licensed by the state they wish to work in, undergo peer review, and pay an application fee.

More than 30 states require geologists to be registered or licensed. Most of these states require applicants (who have earned a bachelor's degree in the geological sciences) to pass the Fundamentals of Geology exam, a standardized written exam developed by the National Association of State Boards of Geology.

Other Requirements

In addition to academic training and work experience, geologists who work in the field or in administration must have skills in business administration and in working with other people. Computer modeling, data processing, and effective oral and written communication skills are important, as is the ability to think independently and creatively. Physical stamina is needed for those involved in fieldwork.

EXPLORING

If this career sounds interesting, try to read as much as possible about geology and geologists. Your best chance for association with geologists and geological work is to join clubs or organizations concerned with such things as rock collecting. Amateur geological groups and local museums also offer opportunities for you to gain exposure to the field of geology.

EMPLOYERS

Approximately 28,000 geoscientists (including geologists) are employed in the United States. The majority of geologists are employed in private industry. Some work for oil and gas extraction and mining companies, primarily in exploration. Others work for business services, environmental and geotechnical consulting firms, or are self-employed as consultants to industry and government. The federal government employs geologists in the Department of the Interior (in the U.S. Geological Survey and the Bureau of Reclamation) and in the Departments of Defense, Agriculture, and Commerce. Geologists also work for state agencies, nonprofit research organizations, and museums. Many geologists hold faculty positions at colleges and universities and most of these combine their teaching with research.

STARTING OUT

After completing sufficient educational requirements, preferably a master's degree or doctorate, the geologist may look for work in various areas, including private industry and government. For those who wish to teach at the college level, a doctorate is required. College graduates may also take government civil service examinations or possibly find work on state geological surveys, which are sometimes based on civil service competition.

Geologists often begin their careers in field exploration or as research assistants in laboratories. As they gain experience, they are given more difficult assignments and may be promoted to supervisory positions, such as project leader or program manager.

ADVANCEMENT

A geologist with a bachelor's degree has little chance of advancing to higher-level positions. Continued formal training and work experience are necessary, especially as competition for these positions grows more intense. A doctorate is essential for most college or university teaching positions and is preferred for much research work.

EARNINGS

Graduates with a bachelor's degree in the geological sciences earned about $39,365 annually in 2005, according to the National Association of Colleges and Employers.

The U.S. Department of Labor reports that the median annual salary for geoscientists was $71,640 in 2005; the top 10 percent earned more than $135,290, while the lowest 10 percent earned less than $39,420 a year. In the federal government, the average salary for geologists in managerial, supervisory, and nonsupervisory positions was $86,110 a year in 2005.

Although the petroleum, mineral, and mining industries offer higher salaries, competition for these jobs is stiff and there is less job security than in other areas. In addition, college and university teachers can earn additional income through research, writing, and consulting. Salaries for foreign assignments may be significantly higher than those in the United States.

WORK ENVIRONMENT

Some geologists spend most of their time in a laboratory or office, working a regular 40-hour week in pleasant conditions; others divide their time between fieldwork and office or laboratory work. Those who work in the field often travel to remote sites by helicopter or four-wheel drive vehicle and cover large areas on foot. They may camp for extended periods of time in primitive conditions with the members of the geological team as their only companions. Exploration geologists often work overseas or in remote areas, and job relocation is not unusual. Marine geologists may spend considerable time at sea.

OUTLOOK

According to the *Occupational Outlook Handbook,* employment of geologists is expected to grow more slowly than the average for all occupations through 2014. Despite this prediction, opportunities in the field are expected to be good because a large number of geologists are expected to retire from the field during the next decade.

Additionally, in response to the curtailed petroleum activity in the 1990s, the number of graduates in geology and geophysics, especially petroleum geology, dropped considerably in the last decade. Relative stability has now returned to the petroleum industry, increasing the need for qualified geoscientists. With improved technology and greater demand for energy resources, job opportunities are expected to be good, especially for those with a master's degree and those familiar with computer modeling and the global positioning system (GPS). Geologists who are able to speak a foreign language and who are willing to work overseas will also have strong employment prospects. In addition to the oil and gas industries, geologists will be able to find jobs in environmental protection and reclamation.

FOR MORE INFORMATION

For information on geoscience careers, contact
American Geological Institute
4220 King Street
Alexandria, VA 22302-1502
Tel: 703-379-2480
http://www.agiweb.org

For information on careers, certification, and scholarships, contact
American Institute of Professional Geologists
1400 West 122nd Avenue, Suite 250
Westminster, CO 80234-3499
Tel: 303-412-6205
Email: aipg@aipg.org
http://www.aipg.org

For career information and profiles of women in geophysics, visit the AWG Web site.
Association for Women Geoscientists (AWG)
PO Box 30645
Lincoln, NE 68503-0645

Email: office@awg.org
http://www.awg.org

For information on student chapters, contact
Association of Environmental and Engineering Geologists
PO Box 460518
Denver, CO 80246-0518
Tel: 303-757-2926
Email: aeg@aegweb.org
http://aegweb.org

For career information and job listings, contact
Geological Society of America
PO Box 9140
Boulder, CO 80301-9140
Tel: 888-443-4472
Email: gsaservice@geosociety.org
http://www.geosociety.org

For information on the Fundamentals of Geology exam, contact
National Association of State Boards of Geology
PO Box 11591
Columbia, SC 29211-1591
Tel: 803-739-5676
http://www.asbog.org

For information on geotechnical engineering, contact
GEOENGINEER
http://www.geoengineer.org

For career and educational information about the geosciences, visit
U.S. Geological Survey
http://www.usgs.gov/education

Geophysicists

QUICK FACTS

School Subjects
Earth science
Physics

Personal Skills
Helping/teaching
Technical/scientific

Work Environment
Indoors and outdoors
One location with some
travel

Minimum Education Level
Bachelor's degree

Salary Range
$28,000 to $71,640 to
$135,290+

Certification or Licensing
None available

Outlook
More slowly than the average

DOT
024

GOE
02.02.01

NOC
2113

O*NET-SOC
19-2042.00, 19-2043.00

OVERVIEW

Geophysicists are concerned with matter and energy and how they interact. They study the physical properties and structure of the earth, from its interior to its upper atmosphere, including land surfaces, subsurfaces, and bodies of water. There are approximately 28,000 geophysicists, geologists, and oceanographers employed in the United States, according to the U.S. Department of Labor.

HISTORY

Geophysics is an important field that combines the sciences of geology and physics. Geology is the study of the history and composition of the earth as recorded by rock formations and fossils. Physics deals with all forms of energy, the properties of matter, and the relationship between energy and matter. The geophysicist is an "earth physicist," one who works with the physical aspects of the earth from its inner core to outer space.

This alliance between the earth and physical sciences is part of the progress that science has made in searching for new understandings of the world. Like the fields of biochemistry, biomathematics, space medicine, and nuclear physics, geophysics combines the knowledge of two disciplines. However, the importance of geophysics goes well beyond abstract theory. Geophysicists apply their knowledge to such practical problems as predicting earthquakes, locating raw materials and sources of power, and evaluating sites for power plants.

THE JOB

Geophysicists use the principles and techniques of geology, physics, chemistry, mathematics, and engineering to perform tests and conduct research on the surface, atmosphere, waters, and solid bodies of the earth. They study seismic, gravitational, electrical, thermal, and magnetic phenomena to determine the structure and composition of the earth, as well as the forces causing movement and warping of the surface.

Many geophysicists are involved in fieldwork, where they engage in exploration and prospecting. Others work in laboratories, where research activities are the main focus. In general, their instruments are highly complex and designed to take very precise measurements. Most geophysicists specialize in one of the following areas:

Geodesists measure the shape and size of the earth to determine fixed points, positions, and elevations on or near the earth's surface. Using the gravimeter, they perform surveys to measure minute variations in the earth's gravitational field. They also collect data that is useful in learning more about the weight, size, and mass of the earth. Geodesists are active in tracking satellites orbiting in outer space.

Geomagnetists use the magnetometer to measure variations in the earth's magnetic field from magnetic observatories and stations. They are also concerned with conditions affecting radio signals, solar phenomena, and many other aspects of space exploration. The data gathered can be most helpful in working with problems in radio and television transmission, telegraphy, navigation, mapping, and space exploration and space science.

Applied geophysicists use data gathered from the air and ground, as well as computers, to analyze the earth's crust. They look for oil and mineral deposits and try to find sites for the safe disposal of hazardous wastes.

Exploration geophysicists, sometimes called *geophysical prospectors,* use seismic techniques to look for possible oil and gas deposits. They may use sonar equipment to send sound waves deep into the earth. The resulting echo helps them estimate if an oil deposit lies hidden in the area.

Hydrologists are concerned with the surface and underground waters in the land areas of the earth. They map and chart the flow and the disposition of sediments, measure changes in water volume, and collect data on the form and intensity of precipitation, as well as on the disposition of water through evaporation and ground absorption. The information that the hydrologist collects is applied to problems in flood control, crop production, soil and water conservation, irrigation, and inland water projects. Some hydrologists study glaciers and their sedimentation.

Seismologists specialize in the study of earthquakes. With the aid of the seismograph and other instruments that record the location of earthquakes and the vibrations they cause, seismologists examine active fault lines and areas where earthquakes have occurred. They are often members of field teams whose purpose is to examine and evaluate possible building or construction sites. They also may explore for oil and minerals. In recent years, seismologists have contributed to the selection of missile launching sites.

Tectonophysicists study the structure of mountains and ocean basins, the properties of the earth's crust, and the physical forces and processes that cause movements and changes in the structure of the earth. A great deal of their work is research, and their findings are helpful in locating oil and mineral deposits.

Volcanologists study volcanoes, their location, and their activity. They are concerned with their origins and the phenomena of their processes.

Planetologists use data from artificial satellites and astronauts' equipment to study the makeup and atmosphere of the planets, the moon, and other bodies in our solar system. Recent advances in this field have greatly increased our knowledge of Jupiter, Saturn, and their satellites.

REQUIREMENTS

High School

A strong interest in the physical and earth sciences is essential for this field. You should take basic courses in earth science, physics, chemistry, and at least four years of mathematics. Advanced placement work in any of the mathematics and sciences is also helpful. Other recommended courses include mechanical drawing, shop, social studies, English, and computer science.

Postsecondary Training

A bachelor's degree in geophysics is required for most entry-level positions. Physics, mathematics, and chemistry majors can locate positions in geophysics, but some work in geology is highly desirable and often required, especially for certain government positions.

Graduate work at the master's or doctoral level is required for research, college teaching, and positions of a policy-making or policy-interpreting nature in private or government employment.

Many colleges and universities offer a bachelor's degree in geophysics, and a growing number of these institutions also award advanced degrees. An undergraduate major in geophysics is not usually required for entrance into a graduate program.

Other Requirements

If you seek employment in the federal government you will have to take a civil service examination and be able to meet other specified requirements.

You should also possess a strong aptitude in mathematics and science, particularly the physical and earth sciences, and an interest in observing nature, performing experiments, and studying the physical environment. Because geophysicists frequently spend time outdoors, you should enjoy outdoor activities such as hiking and camping.

EXPLORING

You can explore various aspects of this field by taking earth and physical science courses. Units of study dealing with electricity, rocks and minerals, metals and metallurgy, the universe and space, and weather and climate may offer you an opportunity for further learning about the field. Hobbies that deal with radio, electronics, and rock or map collecting also offer opportunities to learn about the basic principles involved in geophysics.

Some colleges and universities have a student chapter of the Society of Exploration Geophysicists that you can join. Employment as an aide or helper with a geophysical field party may be available during the summer months and provide you with the opportunity to study the physical environment and interact with geophysicists.

EMPLOYERS

Approximately 28,000 geoscientists (including geophysicists) are employed in the United States. Primary employers of geophysicists are the petroleum industry, mining companies, exploration and consulting firms, and research institutions. A few geophysicists work as consultants, offering their services on a fee or contract basis. Many work for the federal government, mainly the National Geodetic Survey, the U.S. Geological Survey, the Army Map Service, and the Naval Oceanographic Office. Other geophysicists pursue teaching careers.

STARTING OUT

Most college career services offices are prepared to help students locate positions in business, industry, and government agencies. Other job contacts can be made through professors, friends, and relatives. Some companies visit college campuses in the spring of each year to interview candidates who are interested in positions as geophysicists. College career services offices can usually provide helpful information on job opportunities in the field of geophysics.

ADVANCEMENT

If employed by a private firm, a new employee with only a bachelor's degree will probably have an on-the-job training period. As a company trainee, the beginning geophysicist may be assigned to a number of different jobs. On a field party, the trainee will probably work with a junior geophysicist, which in many companies is the level of assignment received after the training has ended.

From a junior geophysicist, advancement is usually to intermediate geophysicist, and eventually to geophysicist. From this point, one can transfer to research positions or, if the geophysicist remains in fieldwork, to *party chief.*

The party chief coordinates the work of people in a crew, including trainees; junior, intermediate, and full geophysicists; surveyors; observers; drillers; shooters; and aides. Advancement with the company may eventually lead to supervisory and management positions.

Geophysicists can often transfer to other jobs in the fields of geology, physics, and engineering, depending on their qualifications and experience.

EARNINGS

The salaries of geophysicists are comparable to the earnings of those in other scientific professions. According to the U.S. Department of Labor, geoscientists (which includes geologists, geophysicists, and oceanographers) earned an average annual salary of $71,640 in 2005. The lowest paid 10 percent earned less than $39,420 per year, while the highest paid 10 percent earned more than $135,290 annually. In 2005, the average salary for a geophysicist working for the federal government was $86,110. Both the federal government and private industry provide additional benefits, including vacations, retirement pensions, health and life insurance, and sick leave benefits.

Positions in colleges and universities offer annual salaries ranging from about $28,000 for instructors to $65,000 for full professors. Salaries depend upon experience, education, and professional rank. Faculty members may teach in summer school for additional compensation and also engage in writing, consulting, and research for government, industry, or business.

Additional compensation is awarded to geophysicists who are required to live outside the United States.

WORK ENVIRONMENT

Geophysicists employed in laboratories or offices generally work a regular 40-hour week under typical office conditions. Field geophysicists work under a variety of conditions and often the hours are irregular. They are outdoors much of the time in all kinds of weather. The work requires carrying small tools and equipment and occasionally some heavy lifting. The field geophysicist is often required to travel and work in isolated areas. Volcanologists, for example, may face dangerous conditions when visiting and gathering data near an erupting volcano.

OUTLOOK

According to the *Occupational Outlook Handbook,* employment of geophysicists is expected to grow more slowly than the average for all occupations through 2014. Despite this prediction, opportunities should be good for geophysicists. The total number of graduates with degrees in the geophysical sciences is expected to remain small and insufficient to meet the moderate increase in industry job openings.

The petroleum industry, the largest employer of geophysicists, has increased its exploration activities, and more geophysicists will be needed to locate less-accessible fuel and mineral deposits and to do research on such problems as radioactivity, cosmic and solar radiation, and the use of geothermal energy to generate electricity. The petroleum industry is also expected to expand operations overseas, which may create new jobs for those who are willing to travel.

The federal government will need more geophysicists to study water conservation and flood control and to assist in space science projects. The growing need to find new sources of energy will undoubtedly make the work of geophysicists more important and more challenging in the next century.

FOR MORE INFORMATION

For information on geoscience careers, contact
American Geological Institute
4220 King Street
Alexandria, VA 22302-1502
Tel: 703-379-2480
http://www.agiweb.org

For information on local meetings, publications, job opportunities, and science news, contact
American Geophysical Union
2000 Florida Avenue, NW
Washington, DC 20009-1277
Tel: 800-966-2481
http://www.agu.org

For career information and profiles of women in geophysics, visit the AWG Web site.
Association for Women Geoscientists (AWG)
PO Box 30645
Lincoln, NE 68503-0645
Email: office@awg.org
http://www.awg.org

For information on careers in geophysics and student chapters at colleges and universities, contact
Society of Exploration Geophysicists
PO Box 702740
Tulsa, OK 74170-2740
Tel: 918-497-5500
Email: web@seg.org
http://www.seg.org

To read the online publication Become a Geophysicist . . . A What?, *visit*
U.S. Geological Survey
http://education.usgs.gov or http://interactive2.usgs.gov/learning
web/explorer/geocareers.htm

Groundwater Professionals

OVERVIEW

Groundwater professionals are different types of scientists and engineers concerned with water supplies beneath the earth's surface. For example, they search for new water sources and ensure safe water supply. There are approximately 8,000 hydrologists employed in the United States.

HISTORY

In addition to the water that can be seen on the surface of the earth, such as lakes, streams, rivers, ponds, canals, and oceans, there is water under the ground, known as groundwater. Groundwater includes things like underground streams and aquifers, which are layers of water-bearing porous rock or sediment. People have been tapping into various groundwater sources for centuries, using the water for everything from drinking to irrigation.

Artesian wells, for example, are used to provide water (including drinking water) in some parts of the world. They are created by boring down into aquifers; the resulting pressure causes water in the aquifer to rise up in the well. Australia has the world's biggest artesian well system; in the United States, artesian systems supply water to parts of the Great Plains and the East Coast.

Like other natural resources, groundwater has been the focus of increasing attention in the United States since the 1970s. The U.S. government has recognized threats to this vital supply of water and passed laws to protect it. At first, people in the field and in related fields were called on to adapt their skills to meeting the new regulations. In recent years, especially as the regulations have gotten more technical and complex, demand for people who specialize in groundwater science has risen dramatically.

A look at the groundwater situation in one state, Florida, demonstrates some of the potential problems. The groundwater in many areas is located not very far under the surface—just a few feet, in some cases. A surging population is drawing heavily on these supplies, threatening to use them faster than they can replenish themselves. Rapid development (farming, mining, construction, industry) offers high potential for disrupting the vulnerable groundwater.

Also, in some cases, below the aquifers in Florida that carry good water are aquifers that carry poor-quality water, high in sulfates. Drawing down too far into the aquifers that have good water might accidentally pull up the bad water from the aquifer below it, or, worse, pull over saltwater from the coast. Once saltwater gets in, that aquifer is probably lost as a source of drinking water.

Another groundwater hazard is the possibility of a fuel, chemical, or other spill on the ground. Hazardous chemicals in these substances can soak through the soil and reach the groundwater, contaminating it. Even good-quality groundwater usually is treated before it is used (although in some places, like outlying rural areas, people drink untreated groundwater, drawing it right out of the ground). Regular water treatment facilities are not designed to handle removal of hazardous substances. That requires special steps, is usually more difficult and expensive than cleaning surface water, and sometimes does not work.

This is, in fact, a national concern. Today, according to the Environmental Protection Agency, some 34 percent of the United States relies on groundwater for its drinking water. At the same time, better methods for detecting contaminants have revealed that contamination of groundwater is more extensive than was previously known.

Legislation (including the Resource Conservation and Recovery Act; the Comprehensive Environmental Response, Compensation, and Liability Act; the Superfund Amendments and Reauthorization Act; and the Safe Drinking Water Act) mandates the cleanup, monitoring, and protection of the nation's groundwater supplies. This direction was strengthened by later amendments to such laws. Recent stricter regulations applying to landfills, for example, acknowledge the potential risks of these operations to groundwater. In particular, seepage from landfills can get into the groundwater and contaminate it. New landfills must have double liners and other features to help prevent seepage; existing landfills have new rules about closing and

Groundwater professionals collect a water sample from a stream. *(Scott Bauer/Agricultural Research Service/U.S. Department of Agriculture)*

capping the landfill to try to stop or minimize seepage. Groundwater monitoring equipment is used to take constant readings of the area's groundwater and determine if any seepage is occurring.

The special problems of groundwater, people's reliance on it, and the laws passed to protect it all have contributed to the growing need for groundwater professionals. Groundwater work is part of the water quality management segment of the environmental industry, which accounts for about one-quarter of all spending on the environment, according to the Environmental Careers Organization.

THE JOB

No one really has the title groundwater professional; instead, it describes any of a number of different positions within the groundwater industry. These include different types of scientists, engineers, and technicians employed in government, private industry, and nonprofit organizations at various tasks designed to ensure safe, effective, and lawful use of groundwater supplies. In earlier times, geologists were often called upon to do groundwater work, and they continue to be important players in the field today. Geology is the science of the earth's history, composition, and structure. Specialties in the groundwater field today include hydrogeology and hydrology. *Hydrogeologists* study the science of groundwater supplies. *Hydrologists* study underground and surface water and its properties, including how water is distributed and how it moves through land. Other professionals in the groundwater industry include chemists, geological engineers, water quality technicians, computer modelers, environmental engineers, chemists, bioremediation specialists, petroleum geologists, and mining engineers.

Employers of groundwater professionals include local water districts, government agencies, consulting firms, landfill operations, private industry, and others with a stake in successful groundwater management. What groundwater professionals do depends on the employer.

Local or regional authorities usually are responsible for ensuring a safe and adequate water supply for people in the area. For example, any time people want to make a new use of water or do something that might affect water in the area (like building a road, drilling a well, or laying a sewer), they have to get a permit. Before it will issue a permit, the authority has groundwater professionals check the site and decide if the use is safe. Typically, geologists do the necessary fieldwork, while engineers handle the actual obtaining of permits.

For a local or regional authority, groundwater professionals might help locate new sources of water in the area, which typically involves surveying the area, drilling for samples, and measuring the capacity of any water reserves found. They find the source of the groundwater and determine its ability to replenish itself if tapped for use, decide how the water would best be used, and make a recommendation to the authority. If the authority approves, a new well system is designed to tap the groundwater, and wells are drilled.

States are big employers of groundwater professionals. What groundwater professionals do for a state depends greatly on what part of the country it is in. The mapping of known groundwater supplies, often using computer modeling to show groundwater flow and possible effects of contamination, is often part of their efforts.

For both state and local or regional authorities, combating the effects of contamination is a critical task. The nature and extent of contamination, combined with the geologic and hydrologic characteristics of the surrounding land, determine whether the water supply is permanently tainted or can be made usable again in the future. Groundwater professionals design systems to reduce or stop contamination.

Another big employer is consulting firms. Regulations for waste treatment and disposal are becoming more and more strict, and that means that more technical expertise is required. Lacking that expertise themselves, many waste generators in the public and private sectors turn to consulting firms for help. Consultants may be called in to help with a hazardous waste cleanup around a landfill, at a Superfund site (an abandoned hazardous waste site), or at another cleanup, or they may help a private industrial company devise a system to handle its waste. Groundwater professionals can be very useful to such consulting firms. For example, if a landfill is leaking waste into a source of groundwater, a groundwater specialist could devise solutions, such as digging new drainage systems for the landfill or building new containment facilities. A groundwater professional with a consulting firm might work close to home or travel to job sites around the country or even around the world.

REQUIREMENTS

High School

At the high school level, you can prepare for a career in groundwater work by taking a lot of science and math. Technology is important in this field, so make sure you have computer skills. Also, focus on developing your writing and speech skills. Reports, proposals, memos, scientific papers, and other forms of written and verbal communication are likely to be part of your job as a groundwater professional.

Postsecondary Training

A bachelor's degree is the minimum requirement for being a professional in this field. According to the Environmental Careers Organization, geology, civil engineering, and chemistry are the most common undergraduate degrees in this field today. Other appropriate majors are engineering, geology, hydrogeology, geophysics, petroleum geology, mining engineering, and other related degrees. Another possibility is a degree in hydrology, although it is not currently offered by many schools. Appropriate course work at the undergraduate level includes chemistry, physics, calculus, groundwater geology, groundwater hydrology, engineering hydrology, and fluid mechanics. It is also a good idea to learn how to do computer modeling, mapping, and related tasks. Undergraduate degrees are sufficient for getting a job doing activities such as on-site sampling and measurement.

A degree in hydrogeology is usually obtained at the master's level. This degree and some experience will place you among the most sought-after workers in the environmental industry.

Certification or Licensing

Some certification programs have been developed to measure experience and knowledge of groundwater science. Both the American Institute of Hydrology and the Association of Ground Water Scientists and Engineers (a division of the National Ground Water Association) offer voluntary certification programs.

Other Requirements

Patience, persistence, curiosity, attention to detail, and good analytic skills are all useful for a groundwater professional. An ability to get along well with others is also important for people working in this profession since you would be likely to work as part of a team and have people to answer to, whether a supervisor, the government, a client, or all three. You would also probably have to be familiar with many regulations, often complex ones.

EXPLORING

You should hold one or more internships while in college (check with your college department for opportunities). You also might be able to find a part-time or summer job with a consulting firm. In addition, check into research opportunities with your professors at your school. You may be able to earn a small salary while gaining experience in fieldwork, compiling and interpreting data, or doing computer modeling. Volunteering for a nonprofit environmental organization might also be an option.

EMPLOYERS

Employers of groundwater professionals include local water districts, government agencies, consulting firms, landfill operations, private industry, and others with a stake in successful groundwater management. Approximately 8,000 hydrologists are employed in the United States.

STARTING OUT

There are many ways to find openings in the industry. One obvious place to start is the want ads, both in the daily newspaper and in various professional journals. Local chapters of groundwater and geological societies sometimes have lists of job opportunities or bulletin boards with important notices. New graduates can also look for work at state employment offices, local or regional water authorities, or the local branches of federal agencies.

ADVANCEMENT

Those starting out with undergraduate degrees are likely to do things like sampling and measuring work. What an employee needs to advance will depend on the employer but probably will include some years of experience plus an advanced degree. It is advisable to keep up on the latest developments in the field through seminars, workshops, and other courses.

Advancement in private consulting firms will likely include promotion to an administrative position, which will mean spending more time in the office, dealing with clients, and directing the activities of other groundwater specialists and office staff. Those working for a local, regional, state, or federal organization may rise to an administrative level, meeting with planning commissions, public interest groups, legislative bodies, and industry groups.

Another option is for groundwater professionals to strike out on their own. With some experience, for example, ambitious professionals might start their own consulting firm.

EARNINGS

Groundwater professionals earn salaries in the upper range of those for all water industry professionals. The U.S. Department of Labor reports that median annual earnings of hydrologists were $63,820 in 2005. The lowest 10 percent earned less than $40,190, and the highest 10 percent earned $102,150 or more.

Benefits depend on the employer. They might include paid vacation, sick days, personal days, health and dental insurance, tuition reimbursement, retirement savings plans, and use of company vehicles.

WORK ENVIRONMENT

Fieldwork might mean going to natural areas to survey the geophysical characteristics of a site. Groundwater professionals may need to take water samples from the monitoring wells near a gas station, fuel storage facility, landfill, sewage treatment plant, or manufacturing company. They may oversee the digging of a new well system or check to see how a new well system is running. Although responsibilities depend on a professional's specific job, some work outside the office and outdoors is frequently part of the job.

In addition to fieldwork, groundwater professionals spend time working in offices. Some professionals, in fact, may spend most or all of their time indoors. Conditions in offices vary by employer, but offices are generally equipped with state-of-the-art technology. Most groundwater professionals work a 40-hour week, depending on project deadlines or unexpected developments in the field.

OUTLOOK

The field of groundwater science remains a promising career choice for motivated, intelligent students. The *Occupational Outlook Handbook* predicts that employment for hydrologists and environmental scientists will grow much faster than the average for all occupations through 2014. The continued growth of our nation's population makes finding and remediating groundwater supplies an even more pressing issue in the 21st century. Private industry must continue to comply with stricter government regulations, including those related to keeping groundwater safe from contamination. Local, regional, and state authorities need to map, develop, and protect their groundwater supplies. Consultants need the specific expertise that groundwater professionals can offer, for clients both in the United States and abroad. Research is needed to develop new ways to treat contaminated groundwater, to prevent spills or leaks, and to develop systems that will make the most of groundwater supplies. All of this means work for groundwater professionals for the near future.

FOR MORE INFORMATION

For the brochure Careers in the Geosciences *and listings of geoscience departments, visit the institute's Web site:*
American Geological Institute
4220 King Street
Alexandria, VA 22302-1502
Tel: 703-379-2480
http://www.agiweb.org

For information on the hydrologic sciences, contact
American Geophysical Union
2000 Florida Avenue, NW
Washington, DC 20009-1277
Tel: 800-966-2481
http://www.agu.org

For information on certification, student chapters, and related organizations, contact
American Institute of Hydrology
300 Village Green Circle, Suite 201
Smyrna, GA 30080-3451
Tel: 770-384-1634
Email: aihydro@aol.com
http://www.aihydro.org

For information on grants, internships, and issues in geoscience, contact
Geological Society of America
PO Box 9140
Boulder, CO 80301-9140
Tel: 888-443-4472
Email: gsaservice@geosociety.org
http://www.geosociety.org

For information on certification, contact
National Ground Water Association
601 Dempsey Road
Westerville, OH 43081-8978
Tel: 800-551-7379
Email: ngwa@ngwa.org
http://www.ngwa.org

For general information about groundwater, visit the following Web sites:

U.S. Environmental Protection Agency
Office of Ground Water and Drinking Water
http://www.epa.gov/safewater

U.S. Geological Service
http://water.usgs.gov/ogw

Marine Biologists

OVERVIEW

Marine biologists study species of plants and animals living in saltwater, their interactions with one another, and how they influence and are influenced by environmental factors. Marine biology is a branch of the biological sciences, and biologists in this area work in myriad industries, including government agencies, universities, aquariums, and fish hatcheries, to name a few. They generally work either in a laboratory setting or in the field, which in this case means being in or on the ocean or its margins.

HISTORY

Marine biologists started to make their study into a real science around the 19th century with a series of British expeditions. In 1872, the HMS *Challenger* set sail with scientists Sir Charles Wyville Thomson and Sir John Murray on the most important oceanographic mission of all time. Over four years, they traveled 69,000 miles and cataloged 4,717 new species of marine plants and animals. Many marine scientists view the reports from this expedition as the basis of modern oceanography.

Before this time, marine scientists believed that sea creatures inhabited only shallow waters. They believed that the intense cold, pressure, and darkness below about 1,800 feet could not support life. Then, in the late 1860s, the HMS *Lightning* and the HMS *Porcupine* made hauls from below 14,400 feet that contained bizarre new creatures.

Scientists began to build precision equipment for measuring oceanic conditions. Among these were thermometers that could gauge the temperature at any depth, containers that could be closed at a

QUICK FACTS

School Subjects
Biology
Earth science

Personal Skills
Mechanical/manipulative
Technical/scientific

Work Environment
Indoors and outdoors
Primarily multiple locations

Minimum Education Level
Bachelor's degree

Salary Range
$25,623 to $50,000 to $96,090+

Certification or Licensing
Required for certain positions

Outlook
About as fast as the average

DOT
041

GOE
02.03.03

NOC
2121

O*NET-SOC
19-1020.01, 25-1051.00

desired depth to collect seawater, and coring instruments used to sample bottom sediments. Scientists also figured out techniques for measuring levels of salt, oxygen, and nutrients right on board ship.

In the 20th century, innovations such as underwater cameras, oxygen tanks, submersible craft, and heavy-duty diving gear that can withstand extremes of cold and pressure have made it possible for marine biologists to observe sea creatures in their natural habitats.

THE JOB

Marine biologists study and work with sea creatures in their natural environment, the oceans of the world and tidal pools along shorelines, as well as in laboratories. These scientists are interested in knowing how the ocean's changing conditions, such as temperature and chemical pollutants, can affect the plants and animals that live there. For example, what happens when certain species become extinct or are no longer safe to be eaten? Marine biologists can begin to understand how the world's food supply is diminished and help come up with solutions that can change such problem situations.

Marine biologists study the remains of a dolphin that stranded on the beach. (Larry Kolvoord/The Image Works)

The work of these scientists is also important for improving and controlling sport and commercial fishing. Through underwater exploration, marine biologists have discovered that humans are damaging the world's coral reefs. They have also charted the migration of whales and counted the decreasing numbers of certain species. They have observed dolphins being accidentally caught in tuna fishermen's nets. By writing reports and research papers about such discoveries, a marine biologist can inform others about problems that need attention and begin to make important changes that could help the world.

To study plants and animals, marine biologists spend some of their work time in the ocean wearing wetsuits to keep warm (because of the frigid temperature below the surface of the sea) and scuba gear to breathe underwater. They gather specimens with a slurp gun, which sucks fish into a specimen bag without injuring them. They must learn how to conduct their research without damaging the marine environment, which is delicate. Marine biologists must also face the threat to their own safety from dangerous fish and underwater conditions.

Marine biologists also study life in tidal pools along the shoreline. They might collect specimens at the same time of day for days at a time. They would keep samples from different pools separate and keep records of the pool's location and the types and measurements of the specimens taken. This ensures that the studies are as accurate as possible. After collecting specimens, they keep them in a portable aquarium tank on board ship. After returning to land, which may not be for weeks or months, marine biologists study specimens in a laboratory, often with other scientists working on the same study. They might, for example, check the amount of oxygen in a sea turtle's bloodstream to learn how the turtles can stay underwater for so long, or measure elements in the blood of an arctic fish to discover how it can survive frigid temperatures.

REQUIREMENTS

High School
If you are interested in this career, begin your preparations by taking plenty of high school science classes, such as biology, chemistry, and earth science. Also take math classes and computer science classes, both of which will give you skills that you will use in doing research. In addition, take English classes, which will help you develop research skills as well as writing skills. And, because you will probably need to extend your education beyond the level of a

bachelor's degree, consider taking a foreign language. Many graduate programs require their students to meet a foreign language requirement.

Postsecondary Training
In college, take basic science courses such as biology, botany, and chemistry. However, your class choices don't end there. For instance, in biology you might be required to choose from marine invertebrate biology, ecology, oceanography, genetics, animal physiology, plant physiology, and aquatic plant biology. You might also be required to choose several more specific classes from such choices as ichthyology, vertebrate structure, population biology, developmental biology, biology of microorganisms, evolution, and cell biology. Classes in other subjects will also be required, such as computer science, math (including algebra, trigonometry, calculus, analytical geometry, and statistics), and physics.

Although it is possible to get a job as a marine biologist with just a bachelor's degree, such jobs likely will be low-paying technician positions with little advancement opportunities. Some positions in the field are available with a master's degree, but most marine biologists have a doctoral degree. Students at the graduate level begin to develop an area of specialization, such as *aquatic chemical ecology* (the study of chemicals and their effect on aquatic environments) and *bioinformatics* (the use of computer science, math, and statistics to analyze genetic information). Master's degree programs generally take two to three years to complete. Programs leading to a Ph.D. typically take four to five years to complete.

Certification or Licensing
If you are going to be diving, organizations like PADI provide basic certification. Training for scientific diving is more in-depth and requires passing an exam. It is also critical that divers learn cardiopulmonary resuscitation (CPR) and first aid. Also, if you'll be handling hazardous materials such as formaldehyde, strong acids, or radioactive nucleotides, you must be licensed.

Other Requirements
You should have an ability to ask questions and solve problems, observe small details carefully, do research, and analyze mathematical information. You should be inquisitive and must be able to think for yourself. This is essential to the scientific method. You must use your creative ability and be inventive in order to design experiments; these are the scientist's means of asking questions about the natural

> # Did You Know?
>
> - Nearly 71 percent of the earth is covered by water—nearly all of which is saltwater.
> - About 80 percent of all living organisms on earth are found in the ocean.
> - Approximately 90 percent of volcanic activity occurs in the earth's oceans.
> - The Pacific Ocean is the world's largest body of water. It covers about one-third of the earth's surface.
> - The Great Barrier Reef is the largest living structure on the planet.
> - The blue whale is the largest animal in the world.
> - Swordfish and marlin are the fastest fish in the ocean.
> - About 50 to 75 people are attacked by sharks each year—with about eight to 12 attacks proving fatal.
> - Only 32 of the approximately 350 species of shark have ever been documented as attacking humans.
>
> Source: MarineBio.org, DiscoverySchool.com

world. Working in the field often requires some strength and physical endurance, particularly if you are scuba diving or if you are doing fieldwork in tidepools, which can involve hiking over miles of shore at low tide, keeping your footing on slippery rocks, and lifting and turning stones to find specimens.

EXPLORING

Explore this career and your interest in it by joining your high school's science club. If the club is involved in any type of projects or experiments, you will have the opportunity to begin learning to work with others on a team as well as develop your science and lab skills. If you are lucky enough to live in a city with an aquarium, be sure to get either paid or volunteer work there. This is an excellent way to learn about marine life and about the life of a marine biologist. Visit Sea Grant's marine careers Web site (http://www.whoi.edu/science/marinecareers/index.php) for links to information on internships, volunteerships, and other activities, such as sea camps.

You can begin diving training while you are in high school. If you are between the ages of 10 and 14, you can earn a junior open water diver certification. When you turn 15 you can upgrade your certification to open water diver.

EMPLOYERS

Employers in this field range from pharmaceutical companies researching marine sources for medicines to federal agencies that regulate marine fisheries, such as the fisheries division of the National Oceanographic and Atmospheric Administration. Aquariums hire marine biologists to collect and study specimens.

After acquiring many years of experience, marine biologists with Ph.D.'s may be eligible for faculty positions at a school like the Scripps Institute of Oceanography or the University of Washington.

Marine products companies that manufacture carrageenan and agar (extracted from algae and used as thickening agents in foods) hire marine biologists to design and carry out research.

Jobs in marine biology are based mostly in coastal areas, though some biologists work inland as university professors or perhaps as paleontologists who search for and study marine fossils.

STARTING OUT

With a bachelor's degree only, you may be able to get a job as a laboratory technician in a state or federal agency. Some aquaria will hire you straight out of college, but generally it's easier to get a paid position if you have worked as a volunteer at an aquarium. You will need a more advanced degree to get into more technical positions such as consulting, writing for scientific journals, and conducting research.

Web sites are good resources for employment information. If you can find the human resources section of an aquarium's home page, it will tell you whom to contact to find out about openings and may even provide job listings. Federal agencies may also have Web sites with human resource information.

Professors who know you as a student might be able to help you locate a position through their contacts in the professional world.

Another good way to make contacts is by attending conferences or seminars sponsored by aquatic science organizations such as the American Society of Limnology and Oceanography or the Mid-Atlantic Marine Education Association.

ADVANCEMENT

Lab technicians with four-year degrees may advance to become senior lab techs after years with the same lab. Generally, though, taking on greater responsibility or getting into more technical work means having more education. Those wanting to do research (in any setting) will need a graduate degree or at least be working on one. To get an administrative position with a marine products company or a faculty position at a university, marine biologists need at least a master's degree, and those wanting to become senior scientists at a marine station or full professors must have a doctoral degree.

EARNINGS

Salaries vary quite a lot depending on factors such as the person's level of education; the type of work (research, teaching, etc.); the size, location, and type of employer (for example, large university, government agency, or private company); and the person's level of work experience. According to the National Association of Colleges and Employers, those seeking their first job and holding bachelor's degrees in biological and life sciences had average salary offers of $31,258 in 2005. The American Society of Limnology and Oceanography reports that those with bachelor's degrees may start out working for federal government agencies at the pay grades GS-5 to GS-7. In 2007 the yearly earnings at the GS-5 level ranged from $25,623 to $33,309, and yearly earnings at the GS-7 level ranged from $31,740 to $41,262. College biology teachers (including those who specialize in marine biology) had median annual salaries of $63,570 in 2005, according to the U.S. Department of Labor. Salaries ranged from less than $33,900 to more than $96,090. Marine biologists who hold top-ranking positions and have much experience, such as senior research scientists, may make more than these amounts.

Benefits vary by employer but often include such extras as health insurance and retirement plans.

WORK ENVIRONMENT

Most marine biologists don't actually spend a lot of time diving. However, researchers might spend a couple of hours periodically breathing from a scuba tank below some waters, like Monterey Bay or the Gulf of Maine. They might gather samples from the deck of a large research vessel during a two-month expedition, or they might meet with several other research biologists.

In most marine biology work, some portion of time is spent in the lab, analyzing samples of seawater or collating data on a computer. Many hours are spent in solitude, reading papers in scientific journals or writing papers for publication.

Instructors or professors work in classrooms interacting with students and directing student lab work.

Those who work for an aquarium, as consultants for private corporations, or in universities work an average of 40 to 50 hours a week.

OUTLOOK

Generally speaking, there are more marine biologists than there are paying positions at present. Changes in the earth's environment, such as global warming and increased levels of heavy metals in the global water cycle, will most likely prompt more research and result in slightly more jobs in different subfields.

Greater need for smart management of the world's fisheries, research by pharmaceutical companies into deriving medicines from marine organisms, and cultivation of marine food alternatives such as seaweeds and plankton are other factors that may increase the demand for marine biologists in the near future. Because of strong competition for jobs, however, employment should grow about as fast as the average.

FOR MORE INFORMATION

The education and outreach section of the AIBS Web site has information on a number of careers in biology.
   American Institute of Biological Sciences (AIBS)
   1444 I Street, NW, Suite 200
   Washington, DC 20005-6535
   Tel: 202-628-1500
   http://www.aibs.org

For information on careers, education, membership, and publications, contact
   American Society of Limnology and Oceanography
   5400 Bosque Boulevard, Suite 680
   Waco, TX 76710-4446
   Tel: 800-929-2756
   Email: business@aslo.org
   http://www.aslo.org

For information on volunteer programs for in-state students and college internships, contact
   National Aquarium in Baltimore
   501 East Pratt Street
   Baltimore, MD 21202-3103

Tel: 410-576-3800
Email: volunteer@aqua.org or intern@aqua.org
http://aqua.org

For information on diving instruction and certification, contact
PADI
30151 Tomas Street
Rancho Santa Margarita, CA 92688-2125
Tel: 800-729-7234
http://www.padi.com

This center for research and education in global science currently runs more than 300 research programs and uses a fleet of four ships to conduct expeditions over the entire globe. For more information, contact
Scripps Institution of Oceanography
University of California-San Diego
8602 La Jolla Shores Drive
La Jolla, CA 92037-1508
Tel: 858-534-3624
Email: scrippsnews@ucsd.edu
http://www-sio.ucsd.edu

For reference lists, links to marine labs, summer intern and course opportunities, and links to career information, check out the following Web site:
Marine Biology Web
http://life.bio.sunysb.edu/marinebio/mbweb.html

For links to career information and sea programs, visit the following Web sites:
Careers in Oceanography, Marine Science, and Marine Biology
http://scilib.ucsd.edu/sio/guide/career.html

Sea Grant Marine Careers
http://www.marinecareers.net

Meteorologists

QUICK FACTS

School Subjects
Geography
Physics

Personal Skills
Helping/teaching
Technical/scientific

Work Environment
Primarily indoors
Primarily one location

Minimum Education Level
Bachelor's degree

Salary Range
$10,000 to $73,940 to
$500,000

Certification or Licensing
Recommended

Outlook
About as fast as the average

DOT
025

GOE
02.02.01

NOC
2114

O*NET-SOC
19-2021.00

OVERVIEW

Meteorologists, or *atmospheric scientists*, study weather conditions and forecast weather changes. By analyzing weather maps covering large geographic areas and related charts, like upper-air maps and soundings, they can predict the movement of fronts, precipitation, and pressure areas. They forecast such data as temperature, winds, precipitation, cloud cover, and flying conditions. To predict future weather patterns and to develop increased accuracy in weather study and forecasting, meteorologists conduct research on such subjects as atmospheric electricity, clouds, precipitation, hurricanes, and data collected from weather satellites. Other areas of research used to forecast weather may include ocean currents and temperature. There are about 7,400 atmospheric scientists employed in the United States.

HISTORY

Meteorology is an observational science: the study of the atmosphere, weather, and climate. The basic meteorological instruments were all invented hundreds of years ago. Galileo invented the thermometer in 1593 and Evangelista Torricelli invented the barometer in 1643. Simultaneous comparison and study of weather was impossible until the telegraph was invented. Observations of the upper atmosphere from balloons and airplanes started after World War I. Not until World War II, however, was great financial support given to the development of meteorology. During the war a very clear-cut relationship was established between the effectiveness of new weapons and the atmosphere.

More accurate instruments for measuring and observing weather conditions, new systems of communication, and the development of satellites, radar, and high-speed computers to process and analyze weather data have helped meteorologists and the general public to get a better understanding of the atmosphere.

THE JOB

Although most people think of weather forecasting when they think of meteorology, meteorologists do many other kinds of work also. They research subjects ranging from radioactive fallout to the dynamics of hurricanes. They study the ozone levels in the stratosphere. Some teach in colleges and universities. A few meteorologists work in radio and televised weather forecasting programs. Networks usually hire their own staff of meteorologists.

Meteorologists generally specialize in one branch of this rapidly developing science; however, the lines of specialization are not clearly drawn and meteorologists often work in more than one area of specialization. The largest group of specialists are called *operational meteorologists*, the technical name for weather forecasters, who interpret current weather information, such as air pressure, temperature, humidity, and wind velocity, reported by observers, weather satellites, weather radar, and remote sensors in many parts of the world. They use this data to make short- and long-range forecasts for given regions. Operational meteorologists also use Doppler radar, which detects rotational patterns in violent thunderstorms, in order to better predict tornadoes, thunderstorms, and flash floods, as well as their direction and intensity. Other specialists include *climatologists*, who study past records to discover weather patterns for a given region. The climatologist compiles, makes statistical analyses of, and interprets data on temperature, sunlight, rainfall, humidity, and wind for a particular area over a long period of time for use in weather forecasting, aviation, agriculture, commerce, and public health.

Dynamic meteorologists study the physical laws related to air currents. *Physical meteorologists* study the physical nature of the atmosphere including its chemical composition and electrical, acoustical, and optical properties. *Environmental meteorologists* study air pollution, global warming, ozone depletion, water shortages, and other environmental problems and write impact statements about their findings. *Industrial meteorologists* work in a variety of private industries, focusing their expertise on such problems as smoke control and air pollution. *Synoptic meteorologists* find new ways

An agricultural meteorologist (right) and an agricultural scientist study a remote-sensing map of a field study of corn and soybean crop yields. *(Scott Bauer/Agricultural Research Service/U.S. Department of Agriculture)*

to forecast weather events by using mathematical models and computers. *Flight meteorologists* fly in aircraft to study hurricanes and other weather phenomena.

The tools used by meteorologists include weather balloons, instrumented aircraft, radar, satellites, and computers. Instrumented aircraft are high-performance airplanes used to observe many kinds of weather. Radar is used to detect rain and snow, as well as other weather. Doppler radar can measure wind speed and direction. It has become the best tool for predicting severe weather. Satellites use advanced remote sensing to measure temperature, wind, and other characteristics of the atmosphere at many levels. The entire surface of the earth can be observed with satellites.

The introduction of computers has changed research and forecasting of weather. The fastest computers are used in atmospheric research, as well as large-scale weather forecasting. Computers are used to produce simulations of upcoming weather.

REQUIREMENTS

High School

You can best prepare for a college major in meteorology by taking high school courses in mathematics, geography, computer science, physics, and chemistry. A good command of English is essential because you must be able to describe complex weather events and patterns in a clear and concise way.

Postsecondary Training

Although some beginners in meteorological work have majored in subjects related to meteorology, the usual minimal requirement for work in this field is a bachelor's degree in meteorology. For entry-level positions in the federal government, you must have a bachelor's degree (not necessarily in meteorology) with at least 24 semester hours of meteorology courses, including six hours in the analysis and prediction of weather systems and two hours of remote sensing of the atmosphere or instrumentation. Other required courses include calculus, physics, and other physical science courses, such as statistics, computer science, chemistry, physical oceanography, and physical climatology. Advanced graduate training in meteorology and related areas is required for research and teaching positions, as well as for other high-level positions in meteorology. Doctorates are quite common among high-level personnel.

Because the armed forces require the services of so many meteorologists, they have programs to send recently commissioned, new college graduates to civilian universities for intensive work in meteorology.

Certification or Licensing

The American Meteorological Society provides three professional recognition programs for meteorologists: the certified consulting meteorologist program, the certified broadcast meteorologist program, and the seal of approval program (to recognize competence in radio and television weather forecasting). Applicants for the certified consulting meteorologist program must meet educational and/or experience requirements, pass an examination, have worked as a professional meteorologist for at least five years, and provide three professional references to attest to their character. Applicants for the certified broadcast meteorologist program must have a degree in meteorology, pass a written examination, and have their work reviewed for "technical competence, informational value, explanatory value, and communication skills." The seal of approval program will be closed to new applicants on January 1, 2009. Contact the society for additional information on certification.

Other Requirements

To be a successful meteorologist, you must be able to work well under pressure in order to meet deadlines and plot severe weather systems. You must be able to communicate complex theories and events, orally and in writing. You must be able to absorb pertinent information quickly and pass it on to coworkers and the public in a clear, calm manner. Meteorologists who work in broadcasting must have especially good communication skills in order to deal with the pressure and deadlines of the newsroom.

EXPLORING

There are several ways that you can explore career possibilities in meteorology. Each year, for example, the federal government's National Weather Service accepts a limited number of student volunteers, mostly college students but also a few high school students. Some universities offer credit for a college student's volunteer work in connection with meteorology courses. The National Oceanographic and Atmospheric Administration can provide details about the volunteer program. The armed forces can also be a means of gaining experience in meteorology.

Arrange for an informational interview with a meteorologist who works at a local airport or college offering classes in meteorology. Your high school guidance counselor should be able to help you set up this meeting. You can also get additional information from organizations, such as those listed at the end of this article.

EMPLOYERS

Atmospheric scientists hold about 7,400 jobs, according to the *Occupational Outlook Handbook*. The largest employer of meteorologists is the federal government. Most of its 2,900 civilian meteorologists work for the National Oceanic and Atmospheric Administration's (NOAA's) National Weather Service stations across the country. The remainder of meteorologists work mainly in research and development or management. Additionally, several hundred civilian meteorologists work at the Department of Defense. Many opportunities are also available in the armed forces and in educational settings. Hundreds of meteorologists teach at institutions of higher education.

Other meteorologists work for private weather consulting firms, engineering service firms, commercial airlines, radio and television stations, computer and data processing services, and companies that design and manufacture meteorological instruments and aircraft and missiles.

STARTING OUT

You can enter the field of meteorology in a number of ways. For example, new graduates may find positions through career services offices at the colleges and universities where they have studied. National Weather Service volunteers may receive permanent positions as meteorologists upon completing their formal training. Members of the armed forces who have done work in meteorology often assume positions in meteorology when they return to civilian life. In fact, the armed forces give preference in the employment of civilian meteorologists to former military personnel with appropriate experience. Individuals interested in teaching and research careers generally assume these positions upon receiving their doctorates in meteorology or related subjects.

Other federal employers of meteorologists include the Department of Defense, the National Aeronautics and Space Administration, and the Department of Agriculture.

ADVANCEMENT

Meteorologists employed by the National Weather Service advance according to civil service regulations. After meeting certain experience and education requirements, they advance to classifications that carry more pay and, often, more responsibility. Opportunities available to meteorologists employed by airlines are more limited. A few of these workers, however, do advance to such positions as flight dispatcher and to administrative and supervisory positions. A few meteorologists go into business for themselves by establishing their own weather consulting services. Meteorologists who are employed in teaching and research in colleges and universities advance through academic promotions or by assuming administrative positions in the university setting.

EARNINGS

The U.S. Department of Labor reports that median annual earnings of atmospheric scientists were $73,940 in 2005. Salaries ranged from less than $37,250 to more than $109,630. The mean salary for meteorologists employed by the federal government was $80,670 in 2005. Meteorologists employed by other professional and technical services earn significantly less, with a mean salary of $46,520, while those working for scientific and development research companies earned mean annual salaries similar to those paid by the federal government, $77,880.

In broadcast meteorology, salaries vary greatly. According to a 2006 salary survey by the Radio-Television News Directors Association, television weathercasters earned salaries that ranged from $10,000 to $500,000, with an average of $63,600. The U.S. Department of Labor reports the mean annual salary for meteorologists working in radio and television broadcasting was $73,140 in 2005.

WORK ENVIRONMENT

Weather stations operate 24 hours a day, seven days a week. This means that some meteorologists, often on a rotating basis, work evenings and weekends. Although most of these weather stations are at airports located near cities, a number of weather stations are located in isolated and remote areas. One of the most remote meteorological posts is in the Antarctic. However, it provides some of the most interesting and relevant data in meteorology. In these places, the life of a meteorologist can be quiet and lonely. Operational meteorologists often work overtime during weather emergencies such as hurricanes. Meteorologists who work in college and university settings enjoy the same working conditions as other professors.

OUTLOOK

According to the *Occupational Outlook Handbook,* employment for meteorologists should grow about as fast as the average for all occupations through 2014. The National Weather Service (NWS) has hired all the meteorologists it needs to staff its recently upgraded weather forecasting stations. The agency has no plans to build more weather stations or increase the number of meteorologists in existing stations for many years.

Opportunities for atmospheric scientists in private industry, however, are expected to be better than in the federal government through 2014. Private weather consulting firms are able to provide more detailed information than the NWS to weather-sensitive industries, such as farmers, commodity investors, radio and television stations, and utilities, transportation, and construction firms.

FOR MORE INFORMATION

For information on careers, education, certification, and scholarships, contact
American Meteorological Society
45 Beacon Street
Boston, MA 02108-3693
Tel: 617-227-2425
Email: amsinfo@ametsoc.org
http://www.ametsoc.org

This government agency is concerned with describing and predicting changes in the environment, as well as managing marine and coastal resources.
National Oceanographic and Atmospheric Administration
14th Street and Constitution Avenue, NW, Room 6217
Washington, DC 20230-0001
Tel: 202-482-6090
Email: noaa-outreach@noaa.gov
http://www.noaa.gov

For a list of schools with degree programs in meteorology or atmospheric science, visit the NWA Web site.
National Weather Association (NWA)
228 West Millbrook Road
Raleigh, NC 27609-4304
Tel: 919-845-1546
http://www.nwas.org

To learn more about the weather, visit the NWS Web site.
National Weather Service (NWS)
1325 East-West Highway

Silver Spring, MD 20910-3280
http://www.nws.noaa.gov

Visit the following Web site for a text and pictorial introduction to the basics of meteorology.
WW2010: The Weather World 2010 Project
http://ww2010.atmos.uiuc.edu

INTERVIEW

Dr. Jenni Evans is a professor in the Department of Meteorology at Pennsylvania State University in University Park, Pennsylvania. She discussed her career with the editors of Careers in Focus: Earth Science.

Q. Tell us about the meteorology program at Penn State.

A. The Meteorology Department at Penn State is the oldest and largest meteorology program in the United States. It has 24 professors and over 400 students and researchers. Each year around 80 students graduate from our department. They go on to be 1) broadcast meteorologists on television, radio, and the Internet; 2) forecasters for the National Weather Service, the military, the National Aeronautics and Space Administration, and private companies; 3) researchers in both government laboratories and private industry; 4) teachers and university professors; 5) advisors to banks and finance companies; and 6) educators in museums and other public service jobs.

Q. Why did you decide to become a meteorologist?

A. As with many of my colleagues, becoming a meteorologist was something of an accident. While some people become fascinated with this science at an early age—often because of a weather event that directly affected their own life—meteorology is largely a "discovery" major: students pursue a more traditional science degree (math or physics, for example), then find that they can use their scientific talents in this field and do something practical and interesting.

That's how it was with me. I was taking undergraduate classes in mathematics, and two of the professors whose classes I found most interesting invited their students to come on a weekend camp-out to see how we could apply mathematics to understanding the atmosphere. I went—and I was hooked!

Q. What are the three most important professional qualities for meteorologists?

A. *A talent for, and interest in, science.* Meteorology is a quantitative science—you have to tell folks how much rain will fall and how cold or warm it will be. And you get to see—every day—if you were right or not. This means that you have to be able to use the science you've learned in a practical way and come up with numbers!

Observational skills. Detective work—being able to look at evidence and to deduce what it means—is a fundamental skill in science.

Communication skills. To be an effective scientist of any kind, you must be able to communicate your results—to tell people what you've found out and why it is important to them.

Q. What advice would you give to high school students who are interested in becoming meteorologists?

A. Do everything you can to hone the skills we've just discussed. Join any clubs that teach you to make observations and to learn from them. Participate in science fairs. Write for the school newspaper and give talks whenever you can.

Q. What advice would you offer meteorology majors as they graduate and look for jobs?

A. Be sure to think about your professional interests, your career goals, and the type of life you want to have as you plan your future. For example, forecasters usually have to work shifts, as it's important to know the latest about the weather 24 hours a day for some industries (for example, planning plane flights, military activities, trucking, shipping, electricity generation, and tourism). If you don't want to have to go to work in the middle of the night, you might want to choose another job in meteorology. Some jobs require you to work on your own, or on a computer, most of the time. Other jobs are mainly team oriented. You should think about how happy you are working on your own or in groups when you are planning your future.

The other important thing to remember is that you can always retrain and change your path. We have had 40-year-old fishermen and retired military troops come back to earn a degree in meteorology and go on and have a new career.

Q. Should students be aware of any changes in the job market? Have certain areas of this field been especially promising (or in decline) in recent years?

A. Meteorology affects almost all aspects of your life: transport, food, education, energy, tourism, and even health. Let's think about each of these: snow, rain, fog, or large waves can affect road, air, and ship traffic. Droughts and floods can affect crop yields. Snow days, and even extreme cold, can cause changes in the school year. Very hot and very cold weather cause a rush on electricity and fuel use, and can lead to electricity shortages or high oil and gas prices. The hurricanes of 2004 and 2005 have resulted in a sharp drop in tourism in the Gulf Coast region of the United States. Warm, wet years can cause increased mosquito populations and can make it possible to spread diseases.

For all of these reasons and more, more and more people have realized that an understanding of meteorology and climate is important to industry. As a result, many industries are starting to employ meteorologists to advise them, from Wall Street to electricity and insurance companies—and many more. These nontraditional jobs are the largest area of growth in meteorology today.

Oceanographers

OVERVIEW

Oceanographers obtain information about the ocean through observations, surveys, and experiments. They study the biological, physical, and chemical composition of the ocean and the geological structure of the seabed. They also analyze phenomena involving the water itself, the atmosphere above it, the land beneath it, and the coastal borders. They study acoustical properties of water so that a comprehensive and unified picture of the ocean's behavior may be developed. A *limnologist* is a specialist who studies freshwater life.

HISTORY

The oceans hold approximately 97 percent of the water on earth and cover more than two-thirds of its surface. Oceans hold food, chemicals, and minerals, yet oceanography is a fairly new science. In fact, according to the Oceanography Society, it was only during the 20th century that we got the first global glimpse of how the oceans work. With such inventions as deep-sea diving gear, scuba, and the bathysphere (a steel diving sphere for deep-sea observation), scientists are undertaking more detailed studies of underwater life. Oceanography includes studying air and sea interaction in weather forecasting, solving sea mining problems, predicting and preventing pollution, studying sea life, and improving methods of deriving foods from the ocean.

It is difficult to project what oceanographers of the future may be doing. They may be living and working on the ocean floor. The U.S. Navy Medical Research Laboratory has conducted experiments with people living under 200 feet of water.

QUICK FACTS

School Subjects
Biology
Chemistry

Personal Skills
Communication/ideas
Technical/scientific

Work Environment
Indoors and outdoors
One location with some travel

Minimum Education Level
Bachelor's degree

Salary Range
$39,365 to $71,640 to $135,290+

Certification or Licensing
None available

Outlook
More slowly than the average

DOT
024

GOE
02.02.01

NOC
2113

O*NET-SOC
19-2042.01

THE JOB

Oceanographers collect and study data about the motions of ocean water (waves, currents, and tides), marine life (sea plants and animals), ore and petroleum deposits (minerals and oils contained in the nodules and oozes of the ocean floor), and the contour of the ocean floor (ocean mountains, valleys, and depths). Many of their findings are compiled for maps, charts, graphs, and special reports and manuals.

Oceanographers may spend some of their time on the water each year gathering data and making observations. People who infrequently go to sea do additional oceanographic work on dry land. Experiments using models or captive organisms may be conducted in a seaside laboratory.

Oceanographers use equipment designed and manufactured in special shops. This equipment includes devices to measure depths by sound impulses, special thermometers to measure water temperatures, special cameras for underwater photography, and diving gear and machines like the bathyscaphe (a submersible ship for deep-sea exploration). In addition to such commonly used equipment, many new devices have been developed for specific types of underwater work. The oceanographer of the future may be using such tools as a hydraulic miner (a dredge to extract nodules from the ocean floor), an electronic beater (a machine used to drive fish), dye curtains, fish pumps, and instrument buoys. New technologies being developed today include satellite sensors and acoustic current-measuring devices.

The oceanographer is usually part of a highly skilled team, with each member specializing in one of the four main branches of the profession. In actual work, however, there is a tremendous amount of overlap between the four branches. *Biological oceanographers* or *marine biologists* study all aspects of the ocean's plant and animal life. They are interested in how the life develops, interacts, and adapts to its environment. *Physical oceanographers* study such physical aspects of the ocean as temperature and density, waves and currents, and the relationship between the ocean and the atmosphere. *Chemical oceanographers* and *marine geochemists* investigate the chemical composition of the water and ocean floor. They may study seawater components, pollutants, and trace chemicals, which are small amounts of dissolved substances that give an area of water a specific quality. *Geological oceanographers* study the topographic features and physical composition of the ocean bottom. Their work greatly contributes to our knowledge and understanding of earth's history.

Books to Read

Crane, Kathleen. *Sea Legs: Tales of a Woman Oceanographer.* Cambridge, Mass.: Westview Press, 2003.

Dinwiddie, Robert, Louise Thomas, and Fabien Cousteau. *Ocean.* New York: DK Publishing, 2006.

Garrison, Tom S. *Oceanography: An Invitation to Marine Science.* 6th ed. Stamford, Conn.: Brooks Cole, 2007.

Hamblin, Jacob Darwin. *Oceanographers and the Cold War: Disciples of Marine Science.* Seattle, Wash.: University of Washington Press, 2005.

Heitzmann, William Ray. *Opportunities in Marine Science and Maritime Careers.* New York: McGraw-Hill, 2006.

Knauss, John A. *Introduction to Physical Oceanography.* 2d ed. Long Grove, Ill.: Waveland Press Inc., 2005.

Lenihan, Daniel. *Submerged: Adventures of America's Most Elite Underwater Archeology Team.* New York: Newmarket Press, 2003.

Miller, Charles B. *Biological Oceanography.* Malden, Mass.: Blackwell Publishers, 2003

Millero, Frank J. *Chemical Oceanography.* 3d ed. Boca Raton, Fla.: CRC Press, 2005.

Parsons, Timothy Richard. *Sea's Enthrall: Memoirs of an Oceanographer.* Victoria, B.C., Canada: Ecco Nova Editions, 2004

Trujillo, Alan P., and Harold V. Thurman. *Essentials of Oceanography.* 9th ed. Upper Saddle River, N.J.: Prentice Hall, 2007.

Oceanography jobs can be found all over the United States, and not just where the water meets the shore. Although the majority of jobs are on the Pacific, Atlantic, and Gulf coasts, many other jobs are available to the marine scientist. Universities, colleges, and federal and state agencies are the largest employers of oceanographers. Mary Batteen is the associate chair of academic affairs in the oceanography department at the Naval Postgraduate School in Monterey, California, a professor in the department, and a working oceanographer. She has many job responsibilities. "I interact regularly with a variety of people: my office staff, faculty, technical staff (usually oceanographers with M.S. degrees), other chairs, the dean, the provost, and many students," she says. "I am responsible for making sure that the oceanography department runs smoothly. As a faculty member, I regularly interact with students when I teach, advise theses, or carry out joint research with them. My major research interest is understanding the coastal circulation off west coasts like

California, Portugal, Morocco, Chile, and Western Australia. Typical research questions I pursue are: Why, at the same latitude, is the water warm off Western Australia and cool off the other west coasts? Why do some coastal currents flow opposite to the prevailing winds? What roles do wind forcing, capes (bays), and bottom topography play in causing eddies to develop off west coasts? To address these questions, I use a combination of numerical models and available ocean observations."

Other employers of oceanographers include international organizations, private companies, consulting firms, nonprofit laboratories, and local governments. Sometimes oceanographers are self-employed as consultants with their own businesses.

REQUIREMENTS

High School

Because a college degree is required for beginning positions in oceanography, you should take four years of college preparatory courses while in high school. Science courses, including geology, biology, and chemistry, and math classes, such as algebra, trigonometry, and statistics, are especially important to take. Because your work will involve a great deal of research and documentation, take English classes to improve your research and communication skills. In addition, take computer science classes because you will be using computers throughout your professional life.

Postsecondary Training

In college, a broad program covering the basic sciences with a major in physics, chemistry, biology, or geology is desirable. In addition, you should include courses in field research or laboratory work in oceanography where available. Graduate work in oceanography is required for most positions in research and teaching. More than 100 institutions offer programs in marine studies, and more than 35 universities have graduate programs leading to a doctoral degree in oceanography.

As a college student preparing for graduate work in oceanography, you should take mathematics through differential and integral calculus and at least one year each of chemistry and physics, biology or geology, and a modern foreign language.

Many oceanography students participate in internships or work as teaching assistants while in college to gain hands on experience in the field. Mary Batteen was a graduate teaching assistant while pursuing her M.S. degree in oceanography. "Besides learning to teach," she says, "I learned on-the-job skills while out on oceanography cruises. While pursuing my Ph.D., I was a graduate research assistant. I learned many computer skills while analyzing oceanographic data and running numerical models."

Other Requirements

Personal traits helpful to a career in oceanography are a strong interest in science, particularly the physical and earth sciences; an interest in situations involving activities of an abstract and creative nature (observing nature, performing experiments, creating objects); an interest in outdoor activities such as hunting, fishing, swimming, boating, or animal care; an interest in scholarly activities (reading, researching, writing); and other interests that cut across the traditional academic boundaries of biology, chemistry, and physics.

You should have above-average aptitudes in verbal, numerical, and spatial abilities. Prospective oceanographers should also be able to discriminate detail among objects in terms of their shape, size, color, or markings.

EXPLORING

Obviously, if you live near coastal regions, you will have an easier time becoming familiar with oceans and ocean life than if you are land-bound. However, some institutions offer work or leisure-time experiences that provide participants with opportunities to explore particular aspects of oceanography. Possible opportunities include work in marine or conservation fisheries or on board seagoing vessels or field experiences in studying rocks, minerals, or aquatic life. If you live or travel near one of the oceanography research centers, such as Woods Hole Oceanographic Institution on Cape Cod, the University of Miami's Rosenstiel School of Marine and Atmospheric Science, or the Scripps Institution of Oceanography in California, you should plan to spend some time learning about their activities and studying their exhibits.

Volunteer work for students is often available with research teams, nonprofit organizations, and public centers such as aquariums. If you do not live near water, try to find summer internships, camps, or programs that involve travel to a coastal area. Visit Sea Grant's marine careers Web site (http://www.whoi.edu/science/marinecareers/index.php) for links to information on internships, volunteerships, and other activities, such as sea camps.

You can help pave your way into the field by learning all you can about the geology, atmosphere, and plant and animal life of the area where you live, regardless of whether water is present.

EMPLOYERS

Approximately 25 percent of those working in oceanography and marine-related fields work for federal or state governments. Federal employers of oceanographers, ocean engineers, marine technicians, and those interested in marine policy include the Department of Defense, the Environmental Protection Agency, the U.S. Geological Survey, and the National Biological Survey, among others. State governments often employ oceanographers in environmental agencies or state-funded research projects.

Colleges or universities employ 40 percent of oceanographers, where they teach, conduct research, write, and consult. The remaining oceanographers work for private industries such as oil and gas extraction companies and nonprofit organizations, including environmental societies. An increasing number of oceanographers are being employed each year by industrial firms, particularly those involved in oceanographic instrument and equipment manufacturing, shipbuilding, and chemistry.

STARTING OUT

Most college career services offices are staffed to help you find positions in business and industry after you graduate. Often positions can be found through friends, relatives, or college professors or through the college's career services office by application and interview. College and university assistantships, instructorships, and professorships are usually obtained by recommendation of your major professor or department chairperson. In addition, internships with the government or private industry during college can often lead to permanent employment after graduation. The American Institute of Biological Sciences maintains an employment service and lists both employers and job seekers.

ADVANCEMENT

Starting oceanography positions usually involve working as a laboratory or research assistant, with on-the-job training in applying oceanographic principles to the problems at hand. Some beginning oceanographers with Ph.D.'s may qualify for college teaching or research positions. Experienced personnel, particularly those with advanced graduate work or doctorates, can become supervisors or administrators. Such positions involve considerable responsibility in planning and policy making or policy interpretation. Those who achieve top-level oceanographer positions may plan and supervise research projects involving a number of workers, or they may be in charge of an oceanographic laboratory or aquarium.

EARNINGS

While marine scientists are richly rewarded in nonmaterial ways for their diverse and exciting work with the sea, they almost never become wealthy by American standards. Salaries depend on education, experience, and chosen discipline. Supply and demand issues along with where you work also come into play. Some examples of jobs in the marine sciences that presently pay more than the average include physical oceanography, marine technology and engineering, and computer modeling.

According to the National Association of Colleges and Employers, students graduating with a bachelor's degree in geology and related sciences were offered an average starting salary of $39,365 in 2005. According to the U.S. Department of Labor, in 2005, salaries for geoscientists (which includes geologists, geophysicists, and oceanographers) ranged from less than $39,420 to more than $135,290, with a median of $71,640. The average salary for experienced oceanographers working for the federal government was $86,110 in 2005.

In addition to their regular salaries, oceanographers may supplement their incomes with fees earned from consulting, lecturing, and publishing their findings. As highly trained scientists, oceanographers usually enjoy good benefits, such as health insurance and retirement plans offered by their employers.

WORK ENVIRONMENT

Oceanographers in shore stations, laboratories, and research centers work five-day, 40-hour weeks. Occasionally, they serve a longer shift, particularly when a research experiment demands around-the-clock surveillance. Such assignments may also involve unusual working hours, depending on the nature of the research or the purpose of the trip. Trips at sea mean time away from home for periods extending from a few days to several months. Sea expeditions may be physically demanding and present an entirely different way of life: living on board a ship. Weather conditions may impose some hazards during these assignments. Choosing to engage in underwater research may mean a more adventuresome and hazardous way of life than in other occupations. It is wise to discover early whether or not life at sea appeals to you so that you may pursue appropriate jobs within the oceanography field.

Many jobs in oceanography, however, exist in laboratories, offices, and aquariums, with little time spent underwater or at sea. Many oceanographers are needed to analyze samples brought to land from sea; to plan, develop, and organize seafaring trips from land; and to teach. Oceanographers who work in colleges or universities get the added benefit of the academic calendar, which provides time off for travel or research.

OUTLOOK

The U.S. Department of Labor predicts that employment for oceanographers will grow more slowly than the average for all occupations through 2014. Although the field of marine science is growing, researchers specializing in the popular field of biological oceanography, or marine biology, will face competition for available positions and research funding over the next few years. However, funding for graduate students and professional positions is expected to increase during the coming decade in the areas of global climate change, environmental research and management, fisheries science, and marine biomedical and pharmaceutical research programs. Although job availability is difficult to predict for several years out, anyone doing good, strong academic work with a well-known professor in the field has good employment chances.

In recent years, the largest demand in oceanography and marine-related fields was for physical and chemical oceanographers and ocean engineers, according to the Oceanography Society. Demand and supply, however, are difficult to predict and can change according to the world market situation; for example, the state of the offshore oil market can affect demand for geological and geophysical oceanographers.

The growth of technology will continue to create and expand job opportunities for those interested in the marine sciences. As ways of collecting and analyzing data become more advanced, many more research positions are opening up for microbiologists, geneticists, and biochemists, fields that were limited by the capabilities of past technology but are now rapidly expanding. All these fields can have ties to the marine biological sciences. In general, oceanographers who also have training in other sciences or in engineering will probably have better opportunities for employment than those with training limited to oceanography.

The Oceanography Society says the growing interest in understanding and protecting the environment will also create new jobs. Careers related to fisheries resources, including basic research in biology and chemistry, as well as mariculture and sea ranching, will also increase. Because the oceans hold vast resources of commercially valuable minerals, employment opportunities will come from pharmaceutical and biotechnology companies and others interested in mining these substances for potential "miracle drugs" and other commercial uses. Continued deep-sea exploration made possible by underwater robotics and autonomous seacraft may also create more market opportunities for underwater research, with perhaps more international than U.S.-based employment potential.

FOR MORE INFORMATION

For education and career information, contact the following organizations:

Acoustical Society of America
Two Huntington Quadrangle, Suite 1NO1
Melville, NY 11747-4502
Tel: 516-576-2360
Email: asa@aip.org
http://asa.aip.org

American Geophysical Union
2000 Florida Avenue, NW
Washington, DC 20009-1277
Tel: 800-966-2481
http://www.agu.org

The education and outreach section of the AIBS Web site has information on a number of careers in biology.

American Institute of Biological Sciences (AIBS)
1444 I Street, NW, Suite 200
Washington, DC 20005-6535
Tel: 202-628-1500
http://www.aibs.org

Visit the ASLO Web site for information on careers and education. For information on membership and publications, contact

American Society of Limnology and Oceanography (ASLO)
5400 Bosque Boulevard, Suite 680
Waco, TX 76710-4446
Tel: 800-929-2756

Email: business@aslo.org
http://www.aslo.org

To purchase the booklet Education and Training Programs in Oceanography and Related Fields, *contact*
Marine Technology Society
5565 Sterrett Place, Suite 108
Columbia, MD 21044-2606
Tel: 410-884-5330
http://www.mtsociety.org

Contact this society for ocean news and information on membership.
The Oceanography Society
PO Box 1931
Rockville, MD 20849-1931
Tel: 301-251-7708
Email: info@tos.org
http://www.tos.org

*For information on undergraduate and graduate programs avail-
able at Scripps Institution of Oceanography, contact*
Scripps Institution of Oceanography
University of California, San Diego
9500 Gilman Drive, 0210
La Jolla, CA 92093-0210
Tel: 858-534-3624
Email: scrippsnews@ucsd.edu
http://www-sio.ucsd.edu

For information about ocean careers and education, contact
Texas A&M University
Department of Oceanography
College Station, TX 77843-3146
Tel: 979-845-7211
Email: info@ocean.tamu.edu
http://www-ocean.tamu.edu

*The IEEE Oceanic Engineering Society is a technical society of
the Institute of Electrical and Electronics Engineering. The OES
Newsletter, with information on the field, can be read online at its
Web site.*
IEEE Oceanic Engineering Society
http://www.oceanicengineering.org

The Scripps Institution of Oceanography Library provides numerous links to career information at this Web site:

Careers in Oceanography, Marine Science, & Marine Biology
http://scilib.ucsd.edu/sio/guide/career.html

Paleontologists

QUICK FACTS

School Subjects
Biology
Earth science
Mathematics

Personal Skills
Helping/teaching
Technical/scientific

Work Environment
Indoors and outdoors
One location with some
travel

Minimum Education Level
Doctorate degree

Salary Range
$35,240 to $71,640 to
$168,000+

Certification or Licensing
None available

Outlook
More slowly than the average

DOT
024

GOE
02.02.01

NOC
2113

O*NET-SOC
19-2042.01

OVERVIEW

Paleontologists study the fossils of ancient life-forms, including human life, found in sedimentary rocks on or within the earth's crust. Paleontological analyses range from the description of large, easily visible features to biochemical analysis of incompletely fossilized tissue. The observations are used to infer relationships between past and present groups of organisms (taxonomy), to investigate the origins of life, and to investigate the ecology of the past (paleoecology) from which implications for the sustainability of life under present ecological conditions can be drawn. Paleontology is usually considered a subspecialty of the larger field of geology.

HISTORY

During Europe's Renaissance, the artist and scientist Leonardo da Vinci, among others, established that fossils were the natural remains of organic creatures, and in the middle of the 17th century, Nicolaus Steno of Denmark wrote a treatise proposing that sedimentary rocks were laid down in layers, with the oldest at the bottom. The physical description of fossils was permissible as long as it did not lead to dissonant conclusions regarding the age of the earth. As an example, the early 17th century saw the naming and characterization of the trilobites, an extinct but very large group of marine arthropods once abundant everywhere in the seas and, as a group, of far greater longevity than the dinosaurs. When fossil evidence was used to advance a history of the earth that contradicted a literal reading of the Bible, however, the penalties were severe.

A paleontologist works on the backbone of a whale skeleton at the Paleontological Research Institute in Ithaca, New York. *(Syracuse Newspapers/Gary Walts/The Image Works)*

The Age of Enlightenment in Europe sped up religion's waning grip on the interpretation of science, and paleontology as a scientific discipline may be considered to have started in the early 1800s. In the young republic of the United States, Thomas Jefferson, then vice president, in 1797 published one of the first papers on American fossil vertebrates; he also named a gigantic ground sloth that once roamed over much of the United States *Megalonyx jeffersonii.* At this time there was considerable congress between natural historians in Europe, Great Britain, and the United States, each eager to learn of the other's latest findings and theories. The 19th century was also the age of the quintessential "gentleman explorer," whose travels overlapped in time with government-sponsored exploring expeditions to all parts of the globe. The number of specimens returned from these expeditions led to the founding of many of the great natural history museums. In the middle of this activity, Charles Darwin boarded the *Beagle* for a multiyear voyage of exploration and natural observation, resulting in his writing *On the Origin of Species by Means of Natural Selection* in 1859, a major contribution to the blossoming of paleontology.

Contemporary paleontology is modeled on an understanding of life-forms as related in extended family trees, some of very ancient origin. In detailing ancestral and modern lineage, paleontologists want to know the precise physical, chemical, and nutritional environment that supported life and what changes in this environment forced some creatures into extinction while allowing others to thrive.

THE JOB

Paleontologists broadly classify themselves according to the life-form studied. *Palynologists* study tiny to submicroscopic life-forms, such as pollen or plankton. Microfossils may be of plant or animal origin and are extremely abundant. *Paleobotanists* study macroscopic fossil plants.

In the animal kingdom, *vertebrate paleontologists* study animals with a backbone, among them the classes of fishes, birds, reptiles, and mammals. Each area of specialization requires extensive knowledge of the anatomy, ecology, and habits of modern representatives of the class. *Invertebrate paleontologists* study animals without a backbone, such as the classes of insects, sponges, corals, and trilobites. Invertebrate paleontologists are especially useful to the oil industry, for fossil plankton taken from drilling cores are an indication of the age of the rocks and of the formations in which oil reservoirs are likely to be concentrated. The mining and minerals industry also hires *stratigraphers* and *petrographers*, who study the distribution and content of rock layers to identify subsurface mineral deposits. These scientists helped to discover rare quarries of limestone in Indiana and other areas. This limestone, composed of the skeletal remains of tiny fossilized creatures, has provided impressive amounts of building material. However, the mining and minerals industry has few positions for paleontologists.

When conducting paleontological research, scientists' analyses begin with careful measurement and anatomical description of fossils, accompanied, if possible, by drawings showing what the three-dimensional creatures may have looked like in life. The fossils then are dated and placed in a physical context. Dating may entail both laboratory analyses and comparisons with fossil beds of known age or a comparison with stratigraphic layers of rock in different formations around the world. In the third step, the fossils and the formations in which they occurred are used to construct a history of earth on either a small, local scale or a large scale. Large-scale events that can be reconstructed from fossil evidence include the uplift, tilting, and erosion of mountain ranges, the rise and subsidence of seas, and movements of landmasses over geological time. In the fourth step, fossils are used as evidence of life to fill in missing links in the fossil record, to revise taxonomic classifications, and to construct the biology of descent of living organisms.

Museum curators are linked to the fourth phase of paleontological analysis, because virtually all contemporary *geology curators* are evolutionists. Museum curators typically hold a doctorate and have done considerable independent research; these positions are highly competitive. Geology curators must raise grant funding to support themselves and a work crew in the field, and some have teaching responsibilities in joint programs of study with universities as well. *Collection managers* in geology usually have a minimum of a master's degree; some have doctorates. *Geology collection managers* study, catalogue, and maintain the museum's collection, ship specimens to external researchers for study, and sometimes participate in fieldwork. Ordinarily there is one collection manager for the geology holdings, but occasionally there is more than one. In that case, the duties may be divided among vertebrate mammals, invertebrate mammals, fossil amphibians and reptiles, fossil birds, and fossil plants. Collection managers are generalists and work as colleagues with curators.

Some paleontologists work as college professors. To teach at this level, they must have a doctorate or be a candidate for a doctorate. Their primary educational responsibilities are divided between teaching undergraduate courses in earth science and advanced seminars in paleontology. In addition to in-class duties, they must also prepare lessons and curriculum, prepare tests, meet with students during office hours, and attend department meetings. They also conduct personal research, focusing on any area of the field that interests them.

Although the preponderance of paleontological research is carried out on land, marine fossil beds are of great interest. The cost of mounting an expedition to extract samples of sedimentary rock from the deep-sea floor usually means that the sponsoring institution must procure sizable support from industry or the government. Some paleontologists work in the oil industry to develop offshore wells; a few find employment with oceanographic institutes.

REQUIREMENTS

High School

Supplement your high school's college prep program with additional courses in the sciences and mathematics, including advanced classes in biology, chemistry, algebra, and trigonometry. Paleontologists rely a great deal on computer programs and databases, so take courses in computers and programming. You will be preparing your findings for publication and presentation, so take English and speech classes. Foreign language classes will also be valuable, as you may be conducting research in other countries.

Postsecondary Training

Paleontology is a subspecialty of geology or, less commonly, of botany, zoology, or physical anthropology. In college, you will major in geology or biology. The college curriculum for geology majors includes mathematics through calculus, chemistry, physics, and life sciences, with additional seminars in the specialty area and in the history of science.

Because paleontology is a specialty area encountered only briefly during the undergraduate curriculum, you should anticipate graduate training. In fact, most scientists in the field find that a doctorate is necessary simply to have time to gain the substantial knowledge base and independent research skills necessary in their field.

Other Requirements

You should be inquisitive, with a natural curiosity about the world and its history. A desire to read and study is also important, as you will be spending many years in school. It is important to have a respect for other cultures, as you may be working closely with professionals from other countries. Good organizational skills will help you in your work with fossils and museum collections. People skills are also very important, as you'll be relying on personal contacts in your pursuit of work and funding.

EXPLORING

An estimated 55,000 amateur rock hounds belong to organized clubs in the United States, and an untold additional number with no formal group membership also delight in fossil hunting in areas open to the public. You should locate and join one of these clubs and/or take fossil-hunting expeditions and visits to museums on your own. Local museums with a strong geology component frequently conduct field trips that are open to the public.

The Midwest and Great Plains states are especially rich in fossil beds, owing to the inland sea that once overlay these areas and whose sediments protected the skeletal remains of creatures from predation or being moved about. Professional geology societies publish brochures on fossil hunting and the kinds of fossils available in different locales. State geological societies, often housed on the main campus of state universities, are excellent sources of information. Earthwatch Institute is an organization that involves people with various environmental projects, including the mammoth graveyard fossil excavation site of Hot Springs, South Dakota.

EMPLOYERS

Most paleontologists work in colleges and universities as faculty of paleontology and geology programs. They also find work in museums and with government research projects. The petroleum industry was once a great source of jobs for paleontologists, but these jobs, though still available, are fewer in number. Some paleontologists are self-employed, offering their expertise as consultants.

STARTING OUT

As an undergraduate, you may be able to work as an intern or volunteer in the geology department of a local museum. You may also be able to participate in fieldwork as a paying member of an expedition. Such an arrangement is usually worked out personally with the expedition leader. These entry-level positions may lead to admission to graduate programs and even to employment after advanced degrees are earned. The American Geological Institute and the Geological Society of America offer some internship and scholarship opportunities.

You will rely mostly on personal contacts when seeking a job after receiving a graduate degree. Networking with others in paleontology, especially your college professors, can allow you to meet those who can direct you to job openings and research opportunities.

ADVANCEMENT

Advancement depends on where the paleontologist is employed. Universities and museums follow a typical assistant, associate, and senior (or full) professorial or curatorial track, with the requirements for advancement very similar: research and publishing, education, and service to the institution. Advancement in museum work may also depend on the acquisition of a doctorate. Advancement in state and federal surveys requires research and publishing. In federal employment and in industry, mechanisms for advancement are likely to be spelled out by the employer. Government-sponsored research and term positions are the least stable avenues of work, because of their temporary nature and dependence on a source of funding that may not be renewed.

Many paleontologists remain active in the field beyond the date of formal retirement, procuring independent research funds to support their activities or developing an unpaid association with a neighboring university to gain access to collections and laboratory facilities.

The low-tech nature of geological fieldwork allows basic field studies to be conducted fairly inexpensively. Others become consultants to geoscientific firms.

EARNINGS

According to the U.S. Department of Labor, all geoscientists, including paleontologists, earned a median annual salary of $71,640 in 2005. The lowest paid 10 percent earned $39,420 and the highest paid 10 percent earned $135,290 or more annually. College earth science teachers (including those who specialize in paleontology) had median annual salaries of $65,720 in 2005. Salaries ranged from less than $35,240 to more than $115,270. A salary survey for the American Association of Petroleum Geologists found that geoscientists working in the petroleum industry with three to five years of experience had average annual earnings of $89,600 in 2006. Salaries increase with a person's years of experience and level of education. Those with 10 to 14 years experience and holding master's degrees averaged $113,400. Those with Ph.D.'s and many years of experience had annual earnings of $168,000 or more.

In 2005, starting annual salaries for graduates with bachelor's degrees in geology and related sciences were $39,365, according to the National Association of Colleges and Employers. Once these highly trained scientists have entered the field, they usually receive excellent benefits packages and ample vacation time and sick leave. In addition, paleontologists who travel to various locations for their research have their travel and accommodations paid for and receive travel stipends from their employer or funding source.

WORK ENVIRONMENT

The day-to-day activities of a paleontologist vary but, in the course of a year, usually involve some mix of fieldwork, laboratory analysis, library research, and grant writing or teaching. In industry, a paleontologist's duties may be defined by the project the company has developed. In academia and in museum work, a paleontologist may be able to define a personal course of research but may have less time for that research because of teaching or administrative responsibilities.

Paleontological study is international in scope and impressive in the sweep of time it commands. Because the fossil-bearing strata of interest to paleontologists occur in widely separated localities, U.S. paleontologists may undertake extensive correspondence or joint fieldwork with colleagues throughout the world. In addition, paleontology is a living science, with new plant and animal species extracted from the rocks every year and corresponding new biological relationships waiting to be explored. The depth and breadth of paleontological study and its ever clearer relationship to contemporary ecological concerns make it an attractive profession for those interested in a larger view of life.

OUTLOOK

More paleontologists graduate each year than there are available positions, and consequently many paleontologists are unemployed or underemployed. Educational opportunities are also diminishing: With decreasing enrollment in all of the physical sciences and increasing pressure to contain costs, colleges and universities are eliminating entire science departments, including geology. Federal and state surveys absorb a small number of new graduates with baccalaureate or master's degrees but cannot accommodate all those seeking work. According to the U.S. Department of Labor, employment opportunities for all geoscientists, including paleontologists, are expected to grow more slowly than the average for all occupations through 2014.

Economics is a determining factor in employment outside of university settings as well. An increasing percentage of the oil used in the United States is imported. As the energy sector moves overseas, fewer jobs are available in the domestic fossil fuels industry. Despite this prediction, the American Association of Petroleum Geologists predicts that a large number of retiring geoscientists will create a need for 200 to 400 new geoscientists (including paleontologists) in the industry each year.

To increase the likelihood of employment, students will find it helpful to pursue high academic standards, including, if possible, independent research and publication during the advanced degree years, cross-training in a related field, such as zoology or botany, and planning a broad-based career that combines knowledge of government activities, industry experience, and teaching and research.

FOR MORE INFORMATION

For information on careers in the geological sciences, as well as information about scholarships and internships, contact
American Geological Institute
4220 King Street
Alexandria, VA 22302-1502
Tel: 703-379-2480
http://www.agiweb.org

For recommended readings, information on internships, and geoscience news, visit the GSA Web site.
Geological Society of America (GSA)
PO Box 9140
Boulder, CO 80301-9140
Tel: 888-443-4472
Email: gsaservice@geosociety.org
http://www.geosociety.org

For general information on paleontology and internships, contact
Paleontological Research Institution
1259 Trumansburg Road
Ithaca, NY 14850-1398
Tel: 607-273-6623
http://www.priweb.org

For information on careers and graduate training, contact
The Society of Vertebrate Paleontology
60 Revere Drive, Suite 500
Northbrook, IL 60062-1591
Tel: 847-480-9095
Email: svp@vertpaleo.org
http://www.vertpaleo.org

INTERVIEW

Robert Ross is the director of education at the Paleontological Research Institution and Museum of the Earth in Ithaca, New York. He discussed his career and the field of paleontology with the editors of Careers in Focus: Earth Science.

Q. Please tell us about the Paleontological Research Institution.

A. The Paleontological Research Institution (PRI) is renowned for its collection (one of the biggest in North America) of over three million fossils and for the paleontology journals (technical magazines for researchers) it publishes that are read by paleontologists all over the world. PRI, which celebrated its 75th anniversary in 2007, is located in the beautiful small town of Ithaca, New York, home to Cornell University, with which PRI is affiliated. In fact, PRI was founded through the vision of a Cornell paleontologist who believed that creating a new organization would help preserve and grow for future generations of paleontologists the amazing research collections and publications that he had begun. PRI is the only world-class paleontological research collection to stand as an independent organization for so many years. It is also notable for being among the few specimen-based organizations to build a major exhibits and education facility so long after their founding; in 2003, PRI opened the 18,000-square-foot Museum of the Earth. Today, PRI employs about 20 full-time employees, many of whom are associated with education, exhibits, and operating the museum.

Q. Why did you decide to become a paleontologist?
A. My interest in paleontology has changed over the years. I grew up collecting abundant fossils in the Allegheny Mountains of southwestern New York State. I loved the anticipation of discovery in looking for fossils, and I enjoyed organizing what I'd found. In school I wrote a couple of long term papers on the history of life and on Mesozoic reptiles. I enjoyed the search for and compilation of information about the organisms and began to get a sense that maybe I too might someday make new discoveries or reinterpret past discoveries.

As I entered college I toyed with the idea of entering engineering, math, or some other science, but in the meantime I found opportunities to get involved with classes and even research in earth and environmental sciences, and this pulled me toward paleontology still further. More advanced classes led me to realize that what I really liked best of all was understanding the large-scale processes—how evolution works and how different numbers of species have evolved and survived in different places. I entered graduate school to study evolution and found that, as much as I loved studying patterns in the data in the lab, I still loved getting in the field—and in fact enjoyed the adventure of traveling to new places to collect samples where few have been before.

Today, I see paleontology from yet another angle: It is connected to many of the most important issues of our day. It informs us how organisms, and the ecosystems they live in, react to climate change and affect climate change; it helps us understand the dynamics of biological diversity and extinction; and it continues to remind us that life and the earth do change through time. We can see the excitement of fossil collecting and the intrinsic appeal of organisms such as dinosaurs in science education, which is the area where I spend most of my time today.

Q. What is one of your most memorable memories of work as a paleontologist?

A. In 2000, a team of geologists and paleontologists from the Paleontological Research Institution went looking for a mastodon skeleton in the muddy bottom of a large pond in a suburban backyard in Hyde Park, New York. A few bones had been recovered accidentally by someone dredging the pond, but we didn't know where to look for other bones, or even if there were any others. At the very end of what may have been our last day of searching, while collecting some additional sediment to study small fossils of vegetation and aquatic invertebrates, my colleague Elizabeth Humbert hit a bone with her shovel. Over the next few weeks we were to find at that spot the entire rest of the skeleton, and in fact it was one of the best-preserved mastodons ever found. The skeleton is now mounted in the Museum of the Earth exhibits, and research continues on the mastodon and other materials from the site. The Discovery Channel made a documentary, *Mastodon in Your Backyard,* about the remarkable find.

Q. What advice would you give to high school students who are interested in this career?

A. The best way to prepare for a career in paleontology is to get a broad education in science and to find opportunities to find and work with fossils. Most paleontologists take a variety of science and math courses in high school, and then major in biology or geology, or both, in college. There are often opportunities in natural history museums to work with fossils as a volunteer or intern. Some areas have active clubs of avocational paleontologists (serious science-oriented fossil collectors). We have had several students in the Ithaca area volunteer at PRI and go on to earn degrees related to paleontology.

Most paleontologists who do research have a Ph.D., though some who primarily do curation, fossil preparation, and education may have a bachelor's and master's degree. Many paleontologists (including myself) really enjoy their college and graduate school years as they pursue their interests in paleontology, so going to school for so many years does not seem like a great burden.

Q. What is the future employment outlook for paleontologists? How will the field change in the future?

A. There have never been a lot of jobs in paleontology, though in the past many paleontologists worked for petroleum companies to help them determine the age and characteristics of rocks that were being drilled. There are also fewer paleontologists doing basic exploratory work for the government than there once were. There do, however, seem to be a stable number of jobs at colleges, universities, and museums. Some paleontologists are hired in part to teach large courses for non-science majors on topics such as dinosaurs and the history of life (I teach such a course at Ithaca College as an extension of my work at PRI).

Perhaps the greatest growth area for paleontology will be application of what we know about the past to environments and climates of the present and future. PRI's director Warren Allmon has written and spoken about this role of paleontology for a number of years. One example is using the fossil record to better understand what ecosystems looked like before human influence and how past change informs how we should approach conservation in the future. This field, "conservation paleobiology," is being promoted by another colleague of mine here at PRI, our director of collections Greg Dietl. Doubtless another important topic of interest will be seeking to understand the long-term response of organisms to climate change, using the fossil record as a guide.

Petrologists

OVERVIEW

Geologists study the overall formation of the earth and its history, the movements of the earth's crust, and its mineral compositions and other natural resources. *Petrologists* focus specifically upon the analysis of the composition, structure, and history of rocks and rock formations. Petrologists are also interested in the formation of particular types of rocks that contain economically important materials such as gold, copper, and uranium. They also study the formation and composition of metals, precious stones, minerals, and meteorites, and they analyze a wide variety of substances, ranging from diamonds and gold to petroleum deposits that may be locked in rock formations beneath the earth's surface.

HISTORY

The field of petrology began to emerge in the early part of the 20th century as a subspecialty within geology. During this period, the mining of oil, coal, precious metals, uranium, and other substances increased rapidly. With the development of the gasoline engine in the late 1800s, oil became the most significant raw material produced in the world, and the study of the earth's rock formations became invaluable to the mining of petroleum. In fact, the petroleum industry is the largest employer of petrologists; most are employed by one segment or another of the mining industry. Petrologists are also used in many other areas of mining and mineral extraction, and they are employed by numerous government agencies.

THE JOB

The major goal of petrology is to study the origin, composition, and history of rocks and rock formations. Because petrologists are intimately involved in the mining industry, they may work closely with the following types of scientists: geologists, who study the overall composition and structure of the earth as well as mineral deposits; *geophysicists*, who study the physical movements of the earth, including seismic activity, and the physical properties of the earth and its atmosphere; *hydrologists*, who study the earth's waters and water systems; *mineralogists*, who examine and classify minerals and precious stones; and *paleontologists*, who study the fossilized remains of plants and animals found in geological formations.

Depending upon the type of work they do, petrologists may frequently work in teams with scientists from other specialties. For example, in oil drilling they may work with geologists and geophysicists. The petrologist is responsible for analyzing rocks from bored samples beneath the earth's surface to determine the oil-bearing composition of rock samples as well as to determine whether certain rock formations are likely to have oil or natural gas content. In precious metal mining operations, petrologists may work closely with mineralogists. They may analyze core samples of mineral rock formations, called mineral ore, while the mineralogists analyze in detail the specific mineral or minerals contained in such samples.

Because the surface of the earth is composed of thousands of layers of rock formations shaped over several billion years, the contents of these layers can be revealing, depending upon the rock and mineral composition of each respective layer. Each layer, or stratum, of rock beneath the earth's surface tells a story of the earth's condition in the past and can reveal characteristics such as weather patterns, temperatures, flow of water, movement of glaciers, volcanic activity, and numerous other characteristics. These layers can also reveal the presence of minerals, mineral ores, and extractable fossil fuels such as petroleum and natural gas.

Petrologists spend time both in the field gathering samples and in the laboratory analyzing those samples. They use physical samples, photographs, maps, and diagrams to describe the characteristics of whatever formations they are analyzing. They use chemical compounds to break down rocks and rock materials to isolate certain elements. They use X rays, spectroscopic examination, electron microscopes, and other sophisticated means of testing and analyzing samples to isolate the specific components of various minerals and elements within the samples in order to draw conclusions from their analyses.

REQUIREMENTS

High School
If you are interested in a career in petrology, you should be aware that you will need an extensive education. Begin preparing yourself for this education by taking college prep courses while in high school. It will be important to focus your studies on the sciences, such as earth science, biology, chemistry, and physics, and on mathematics, including algebra, geometry, and calculus. You should also take speech and English classes to hone your research, writing, and speaking skills. In addition, take computer science, geography, and history classes.

Postsecondary Training
Most professional positions in the field of petrology require a master's degree or a doctorate. Although individuals without these degrees can technically become petrologists, advances in the field and the profession's requirements will make it extremely difficult to enter the field without a graduate degree.

In college, you should concentrate your studies on the earth and physical sciences, geology, paleontology, mineralogy, and, of course, physics, chemistry, and mathematics. Because petrologists frequently analyze large volumes of data and write reports on such data, courses in computer science and English composition are advisable. Many students begin their careers in petrology by first majoring in geology or paleontology as an undergraduate and then, as graduate students, enter formal training in the field of petrology.

The two major professional associations that provide information and continuing education to petrologists are the Geological Society of America and the American Association of Petroleum Geologists. The American Geological Institute directory can provide information concerning educational requirements for petrologists as well as schools offering formal training in this area.

Certification or Licensing
Although no special certification exists for the field of petrology, several states require the registration of petrologists, and government petrologists may be required to take the civil service examination.

Other Requirements

Requirements for this profession depend in large part upon the segment or subspecialty of the profession you choose. In some cases, petrologists work within a confined geographic area and spend most of their time in laboratories. In other instances, petrologists are called upon to travel throughout the United States and even overseas. Extensive travel is often required if you are working for a multinational oil company or other mining operation where you need to be available on short notice to analyze samples in various localities. Where important mining operations are undertaken, petrologists may be required to analyze rocks, ore, core samples, or other materials on short notice and under deadline pressure.

As with other scientific disciplines, teamwork is often an essential part of the job. Petrologists must be able to understand and relate to geologists, paleontologists, mineralogists, and other scientific experts; they must also be able to relate to and communicate their findings to supervisory personnel who may lack a strong technical background.

If you are considering petrology, you must be able to work well with others, as well as independently, on various projects. You should also enjoy travel and the outdoors.

EXPLORING

To explore your interest in this field, join your school's science club and any local rock-hunting groups to become actively involved in science. Talk to your science teachers about petrology; they may know of a petrologist you can interview to find out about his or her experiences and education. Your high school guidance counselor may also be able to help you arrange such an informational interview. Petrologists may be found in universities and colleges that offer courses in geology and petrology, in certain government offices and field offices, and especially throughout the mining, oil, and natural gas industries.

Both geologists and petrologists require assistance in their work, and it is possible to obtain summer jobs and part-time employment in certain parts of the country where mining or oil exploration activities are taking place. If such work is unavailable to you, try to get a part-time or summer job at a museum in your area that has a geology department, rock collections, or mineral collections. Volunteering at museums is also possible.

For further information about the field of petrology and about various conferences in the geological professions, contact the organizations listed at the end of this article.

EMPLOYERS

Because much of the practice of petrology relates to the extraction of minerals, fossil fuels, metals, and natural resources, most petrologists work for petroleum and mining companies. Their work includes mining on the earth's surface, beneath the earth's surface, and under the ocean floor (in the case of offshore oil drilling, for example). Other petrologists work for federal, state, and local governments. In the federal branch, petrologists are often employed by the Environmental Protection Agency, the Department of Agriculture, the Department of Energy, the Department of Defense, the Department of Commerce, and the Department of the Interior. The largest government employer is the U.S. Geological Survey, a branch of the U.S. Department of the Interior. Other petrologists teach earth science in high schools, teach geology and petrology courses in colleges and universities, or work as consultants. In fact, the consulting industry is the most active employer of petrologists and will probably remain so.

The field of petrology is open to a number of activities and subspecialties, and during their careers petrologists normally specialize in one area.

STARTING OUT

Both the federal government and state governments employ petrologists in various agencies. Thus, if you are undertaking graduate programs in petrology, you should contact both state civil service agencies in your respective state and the federal Office of Personnel Management (OPM). Federal agencies generally notify the OPM when they wish to fill vacancies in various positions and when new positions are created. The OPM has job information centers located in major cities throughout the United States, as well as a Web site, http://www.usajobs.opm.gov, that lists job openings. You can also obtain job information through the employment offices in your state's capital.

Although industrial firms do engage in campus recruiting, particularly for master's and doctoral level job applicants, less recruiting is occurring now than in the past. Therefore, job seekers should not hesitate to contact oil exploration companies, mining companies, and other organizations directly. It is always a good idea to contact geologists and petrologists directly in various companies to learn about opportunities.

Part-time employment is available to geologists and petrologists in both private industry and various federal and state agencies. In some cases, agencies use volunteer students and scientists and pay only some expenses rather than a full salary. This arrangement may still be a good way to gain experience and to meet professionals in the field.

If you wish to teach petrology, you should consult college and university employment listings. For graduate students in the field, a limited number of part-time jobs as well as instructor-level jobs are available.

Note that junior high schools and high schools generally need more instructors in petrology and related geosciences than do colleges. This reflects the fact that many high schools are beginning to offer a broader range of science courses. Individuals with a master's or doctoral degree are likely to be qualified to teach a variety of courses at the high school level, including earth science, physics, chemistry, mathematics, and biology.

ADVANCEMENT

Because the level of competition in this field is keen and the oil industry is subject to fluctuation, those wishing to enter the petrology profession must think seriously about obtaining the highest level of education possible.

Advancement in the field generally involves spending a number of years as a staff scientist and then taking on supervisory and managerial responsibilities. The abilities to work on a team, to perform accurate and timely research, and to take charge of projects are all important for advancement in this field.

Because petrology, geology, and mineralogy are sciences that overlap, especially in industry, it is possible for petrologists to become mineralogists or geologists under the right circumstances. The fact that the three disciplines are intimately related can work to a person's advantage, particularly in changing economic times.

EARNINGS

Earnings for petrologists vary according to a person's educational attainment, experience, and ability. In 2005, according to the National Association of Colleges and Employers, graduates holding a bachelor's degree in geology and related sciences received beginning salary offers averaging $39,365 a year. The U.S. Department of Labor reports that the median annual salary for geoscientists, except hydrologists and geographers, was $71,640 in 2005. The lowest paid 10 percent earned less than $39,420, while the highest paid 10 percent earned more than $135,290. Geoscientists earned the following mean annual earnings by employer: power generation and supply, $91,970; federal government, $86,110; and state government, $51,310. A salary survey for the American Association of Petroleum Geologists found that in 2006 petroleum geologists with three to five years of work experience had average salaries of $89,600; with 10 to 14 years of experience, $111,500; and 25-plus years of experience, $149,900.

Petrologists employed by oil companies or consulting firms generally start at somewhat higher salaries than those who work for the government, but private industry favors those with master's or doctoral degrees.

Many petrologists are eligible to receive fringe benefits, such as life and health insurance, paid vacations, and pension plans.

WORK ENVIRONMENT

Because the field of petrology involves a considerable amount of testing of rocks, ores, and other materials at mining sites and other types of geological sites, petrologists can expect to travel a considerable amount. In some cases, petrologists must travel back and forth from a field site to a laboratory several times while conducting a series of tests. If petrologists are working on exploratory investigations of a potential site for fuel, they may be at a remote location for weeks or months, until the data collected are sufficient to return to the laboratory. The conditions may be arduous, and there may be little to do during leisure time.

The hours and working conditions of petrologists vary, but petrologists working in the field can generally expect long hours. Petrologists, geologists, and mineralogists frequently work in teams, and petrologists may work under the supervision of a head geologist, for example. In private industry, they also frequently work with mining engineers, mine supervisors, drilling supervisors, and others who are all part of a larger mining or drilling operation.

OUTLOOK

The U.S. Department of Labor reports that employment opportunities for geoscientists will grow more slowly than the average for all occupations through 2014. Despite this prediction, opportunities for petrologists—especially those who are employed by petroleum and mining companies—will be good. A worldwide escalation in oil prices has spurred an increase in oil drilling and exploration.

As a result, the number of new jobs in this field has increased, and the number of students who graduate with degrees in petrology or geology is on the rise. Additionally, environmental regulations will create a need for these scientists in environmental protection and reclamation work.

FOR MORE INFORMATION

For information on careers in petroleum geology, contact
American Association of Petroleum Geologists
PO Box 979
Tulsa, OK 74101-0979
Tel: 800-364-2274
http://www.aapg.org

For information on careers, contact
American Geological Institute
4220 King Street
Alexandria, VA 22302-1502
Tel: 703-379-2480
http://www.agiweb.org

Association of Environmental and Engineering Geologists
PO Box 460518
Denver, CO 80246-0518
Tel: 303-757-2926
Email: aeg@aegweb.org
http://aegweb.org

For information on internships, contact
Geological Society of America
PO Box 9140
Boulder, CO 80301-9140
Tel: 888-443-4472
Email: gsaservice@geosociety.org
http://www.geosociety.org

Range Managers

QUICK FACTS

School Subjects
Biology
Earth science

Personal Skills
Leadership/management
Technical/scientific

Work Environment
Indoors and outdoors
Primarily multiple locations

Minimum Education Level
Bachelor's degree

Salary Range
$24,677 to $37,390 to
$58,162+

Certification or Licensing
Voluntary

Outlook
More slowly than the average

DOT
040

GOE
02.03.02

NOC
2223

O*NET-SOC
19-1031.02

OVERVIEW

Range managers work to maintain and improve grazing lands on public and private property. They research, develop, and carry out methods to improve and increase the production of forage plants, livestock, and wildlife without damaging the environment; develop and carry out plans for water facilities, erosion control, and soil treatments; restore rangelands that have been damaged by fire, pests, and undesirable plants; and manage the upkeep of range improvements, such as fences, corrals, and reservoirs.

HISTORY

Early in history, primitive peoples grazed their livestock wherever forage was plentiful. As the supply of grass and shrubs became depleted, they simply moved on, leaving the stripped land to suffer the effects of soil erosion. When civilization grew and the nomadic tribes began to establish settlements, people began to recognize the need for conservation and developed simple methods of land terracing, irrigation, and the rotation of grazing lands.

Much the same thing happened in the United States. The rapid expansion across the continent in the 19th century was accompanied by the destruction of plant and animal life and the abuse of the soil. Because the country's natural resources appeared inexhaustible, the cries of alarm that came from a few concerned conservationists went unheeded. It was not until after 1890 that conservation became a national policy. Today several state and federal agencies are actively involved in protecting the nation's soil, water, forests, and wildlife.

Rangelands cover more than a billion acres of the United States, mostly in the western states and Alaska. Many natural resources are found there: grass and shrubs for animal grazing, wildlife habitats, water from vast watersheds, recreation facilities, and valuable mineral and energy resources. In addition, rangelands are used by scientists who conduct studies of the environment.

THE JOB

Range managers are sometimes known as *range scientists, range ecologists,* or *range conservationists.* Their goal is to maximize range resources without damaging the environment. They accomplish this in a number of ways.

To help ranchers attain optimum production of livestock, range managers study the rangelands to determine the number and kind of livestock that can be most profitably grazed, the grazing system to use, and the best seasons for grazing. The system they recommend must be designed to conserve the soil and vegetation for other uses, such as wildlife habitats, outdoor recreation, and timber.

Grazing lands must continually be restored and improved. Range managers study plants to determine which varieties are best suited to a particular range and to develop improved methods for reseeding. They devise biological, chemical, or mechanical ways of controlling undesirable and poisonous plants, and they design methods of protecting the range from grazing damage.

Range managers also develop and help carry out plans for water facilities, structures for erosion control, and soil treatments. They are responsible for the construction and maintenance of such improvements as fencing, corrals, and reservoirs for stock watering.

Although a great deal of range managers' time is spent outdoors, they also spend some time in offices, consulting with other conservation specialists, preparing written reports, and doing administrative work.

Rangelands have more than one use, so range managers often work in such closely related fields as wildlife and watershed management, forest management, and recreation. *Soil conservationists* and *naturalists* are concerned with maintaining ecological balance both on the range and in the forest preserves.

REQUIREMENTS

High School

If you are interested in pursuing a career in range management, you should begin planning your education early. Since you will need a college degree for this work, take college preparatory classes in high school. Your class schedule should include the sciences, such as earth science, biology, and chemistry. Take mathematics and economics classes. Any courses that teach you to work with a computer will also be beneficial. You will frequently use this tool in your career to keep records, file reports, and do planning. English courses will also help you develop your research, writing, and reading skills. You will need all of these skills in college and beyond.

Postsecondary Training

The minimum educational requirement for range managers is usually a bachelor's degree in range management or range science. To be hired by the federal government, you will need at least 42 credit hours in plant, animal, or soil sciences and natural resources management courses, including at least 18 hours in range management. If you would like a teaching or research position, you will need a graduate degree in range management. Advanced degrees may also prove helpful for advancement in other jobs.

To receive a bachelor's degree in range management, students must have acquired a basic knowledge of biology, chemistry, physics, mathematics, and communication skills. Specialized courses in range management combine plant, animal, and soil sciences with the principles of ecology and resource management. Students are also encouraged to take electives, such as economics, forestry, hydrology, agronomy, wildlife, and computer science.

While a number of schools offer some courses related to range management, only nine colleges and universities have degree programs in range management or range science that are accredited by the Society of Range Management. More than 40 other schools offer course work available in a discipline with a range management or range science option.

Certification or Licensing

The Society for Range Management offers certification as a certified range management consultant or a certified professional in rangeland management. These are voluntary certifications but demonstrate a professional's commitment to the field and the high quality of his or her work. Requirements for certification include having a bachelor's degree and at least five years of experience in the field as well as passing a written exam.

Other Requirements

Along with their technical skills, range managers must be able to speak and write effectively and to work well with others. Range managers need to be self-motivated and flexible. They are generally persons who do not want the restrictions of an office setting and a rigid schedule. They should have a love for the outdoors as well as good health and physical stamina for the strenuous activity that this occupation requires.

EXPLORING

As a high school student, you can test your appetite for outdoor work by applying for summer jobs on ranches or farms. Other ways of exploring this occupation include a field trip to a ranch or interviews with or lectures by range managers, ranchers, or conservationists. Any volunteer work with conservation organizations—large or small—will give you an idea of what range managers do and will help you when you apply to colleges and for employment.

As a college student, you can get more direct experience by applying for summer jobs in range management with such federal agencies as the Forest Service, the Natural Resources Conservation Service (NRCS), and the Bureau of Land Management (BLM). This experience may better qualify you for jobs when you graduate.

EMPLOYERS

The majority of range managers are employed by the federal government in the BLM or the NRCS. State governments employ range managers in game and fish departments, state land agencies, and extension services.

In private industry, the number of range managers is increasing. They work for coal and oil companies to help reclaim mined areas, for banks and real estate firms to help increase the revenue from landholdings, and for private consulting firms and large ranches. Some range managers with advanced degrees teach and do research at colleges and universities. Others work overseas with U.S. and United Nations agencies and with foreign governments.

STARTING OUT

The usual way to enter this occupation is to apply directly to the appropriate government agencies. People interested in working for the federal government may contact the Department of Agriculture's Forest Service or the NRCS, or the Department of the Interior's Bureau of Indian Affairs or the BLM. Others may apply to local state employment offices for jobs in state land agencies, game and fish departments, or agricultural extension services. Your college career services office should have listings of available jobs.

ADVANCEMENT

Range managers may advance to administrative positions in which they plan and supervise the work of others and write reports. Others may go into teaching or research. An advanced degree is often necessary for the higher-level jobs in this field. Another way for range managers to advance is to enter business for themselves as range management consultants or ranchers.

EARNINGS

According to the U.S. Department of Labor, in 2005, most bachelor's degree graduates entering federal government jobs as foresters, range managers, or soil conservationists started at $24,677 or $30,567, depending on academic achievement. Those with a master's degree could start at $37,390 or $45,239, and those with doctorates could start at $54,221. The average federal salary for rangeland managers was $58,162 in 2005.

State governments and private companies pay their range managers salaries that are about the same as those paid by the federal government. Range managers are also eligible for paid vacations and sick days, health and life insurance, and other benefits.

WORK ENVIRONMENT

Range managers, particularly those just beginning their careers, spend a great deal of time on the range. That means they must work outdoors in all kinds of weather. They usually travel by car or small plane, but in rough country they use four-wheel-drive vehicles or get around on horseback or on foot. When riding the range, managers may spend a considerable amount of time away from home, and the work is often quite strenuous.

As range managers advance to administrative jobs, they spend more time working in offices, writing reports, and planning and supervising the work of others. Range managers may work alone or under direct supervision; often they work as part of a team. In any case, they must deal constantly with people—not only their superiors and coworkers but with the general public, ranchers, government officials, and other conservation specialists.

OUTLOOK

This is a small occupation, and most of the openings will arise when older, experienced range managers retire or leave the occupation. The

U.S. Department of Labor predicts that job growth will be slower than the average for all occupations through 2014 for conservation scientists and foresters, a category that includes range managers. The need for range managers should be stimulated by a growing demand for wildlife habitats, recreation, and water as well as by an increasing concern for the environment. A greater number of large ranches will employ range managers to improve range management practices and increase output and profitability. Range specialists will also be employed in larger numbers by private industry to reclaim lands damaged by oil and coal exploration. A small number of new jobs will result from the need for range and soil conservationists to provide technical assistance to owners of grazing land through the NRCS.

An additional demand for range managers could be created by the conversion of rangelands to other purposes, such as wildlife habitats and recreation. Federal employment for these activities, however, depends on the passage of legislation concerning the management of range resources, an area that is always controversial. Smaller budgets may also limit employment growth in this area.

FOR MORE INFORMATION

Career and education information may be obtained from
National Recreation and Park Association
22377 Belmont Ridge Road
Ashburn, VA 20148-4501
Tel: 703-858-0784
Email: info@nrpa.org
http://www.nrpa.org

This organization has career, education, scholarship, and certification information. Student membership is also available through its International Student Conclave.
Society for Range Management
10030 West 27th Avenue
Wheat Ridge, CO 80215-6601
Tel: 303-986-3309
Email: srmweb@rangelands.org
http://www.rangelands.org

For information about career opportunities in the federal government, contact
Bureau of Indian Affairs
1849 C Street, NW
Washington, DC 20240-0001

Tel: 202-208-3100
http://www.doi.gov

Bureau of Land Management
1849 C Street, Room 406-LS
Washington, DC 20240-0001
Tel: 202-452-5125
http://www.blm.gov

National Park Service
1849 C Street, NW
Washington, DC 20240-0001
Tel: 202-208-5391
http://www.nps.gov

Natural Resources Conservation Service
Attn: Legislative and Public Affairs Division
PO Box 2890
Washington, DC 20013-2890
Tel: 202-720-3210
http://www.nrcs.usda.gov

U.S. Forest Service
1400 Independence Avenue, SW
Washington, DC 20250-0003
Tel: 202-205-8333
http://www.fs.fed.us

INTERVIEW

Jack Hamby works as a range management professional for the Bureau of Land Management in Washington, D.C. He discussed his career with the editors of Careers in Focus: Earth Science.

Q. How long have you been a range professional?
A. I have worked for the Bureau of Land Management (BLM) for almost 17 years. I started as a cooperative education student while I was still in college. However, I am also a second-generation BLM employee. My father was a range conservationist when I was growing up.

Q. Where have you worked in your career?
A. I currently work in the Washington, D.C., headquarters office as a deputy division chief (an "assistant manager" type) in the

Division of Rangeland Resources. I began my career as a range-land management specialist in Susanville, California, moved into the Wild Horse and Burro Program in Tonopah, Nevada, and then to chief of operations in Battle Mountain, Nevada. I have also completed various short-term assignments as a wildlife biologist, field office manager, division chief, monitoring program lead, public affairs specialist, forester, etc.

Q. When and how did you decide to get into the field?

A. I spent the first two years of college completing the basic classes—just like everyone else. However, in looking to declare a major, my interest lay in outdoor activities, and while searching career fields I found there were 45 people in the forestry program, 50 in the wildlife program, and only four declared range majors. I saw a few job openings and figured I had a better chance at securing a full-time job in the range field than anything else. The more classes I took, the more I enjoyed the field. To be a range manager, you must also have knowledge of the other outdoor disciplines including wildlife, forestry, recreation, plants, soils, hydrology, geology, and animal science. Getting a job was not easy. I filled out a lot of applications before I was offered my first job (ironically, I received two phone calls from potential employers on the same day).

Q. What advice would you offer high school students who are interested in outdoor-related careers?

A. Focus on your major, but be general in your studies. Uncle Sam is looking for people who can wear a myriad of hats—who are experts in one field, but who can participate across several disciplines. Also, remember to include some social aspects in your curriculum. Having a 4.0 G.P.A. is great, but without participation in clubs and social activities, you can come across as a one-sided person. We conducted a study at the university I attended and found out that businesses wanted well-rounded people and not just straight-A students. Networking is also extremely important. I hate to say this, but it is often more important "who you know" than "what you know."

Q. What are the three most important professional qualities for range management professionals?

A. Wow, this is tough. I would say decision making is probably number one. The ability to make a decision using the best possible information is important. You need to be able to manage risk in the decision-making process. A close second is communication—both written and oral. A single typo in a job application can send your application to the bottom of the pile. The ability to get your message across (without being verbose) is paramount in any modern-day endeavor. Number three would have to be enthusiasm/passion and the willingness to go the extra mile. Everyone wants to be around people who are excited, confident, and willing to help others. To be noticed (and hired), you must be willing to work twice as hard (and smarter) than the next person. These may not be professional qualities in the academic sense, but when I hire a person (and I have hired or approved for hire a lot of people), these qualities are weighted heavier than scholastic achievements.

Q. What do you dislike and like most about your job?

A. I dislike all of the administrative paperwork. It detracts from the core mission, but it is also a necessary evil so I don't let it get to me. While I would rather be doing more on-the-ground work, I do the paperwork because I have to.

What I really like is that I never do the exact same thing every day. There is a tremendous variety of work to do. For a person who is looking for a job that will never be boring—for a career in which you can make your own way and achieve every goal you set in front of you—I highly recommend the BLM. I cannot see myself doing anything else.

Q. What is the future employment for range management professionals?

A. BLM's forecast is that 35 percent of its employees will be eligible to retire in the next four years. It is predicted that approximately half of these people will leave in the next 18 months. There is a tremendous employment opportunity in the not-too-distant future.

Science Writers

OVERVIEW

Science writers translate technical scientific information so it can be disseminated to the general public and professionals in the field. Science writers research, interpret, write, and edit scientific information. Their work often appears in books, technical studies and reports, magazine and trade journal articles, newspapers, company newsletters, and on Web sites and may be used for radio and television broadcasts.

HISTORY

The skill of writing has existed for thousands of years. Papyrus fragments with writing by ancient Egyptians date from about 3000 B.C., and archaeological findings show that the Chinese had developed books by about 1300 B.C. A number of technical obstacles had to be overcome before printing and the writing profession progressed.

The modern publishing age began in the 18th century. Printing became mechanized, and the novel, magazine, and newspaper developed. Developments in the printing trades, photoengraving, retailing, and the availability of capital produced a boom in newspapers and magazines in the 19th century. Further mechanization in the printing field, such as the use of the Linotype machine, high-speed rotary presses, and special color-reproduction processes, set the stage for still further growth in the book, newspaper, and magazine industry.

The broadcasting industry has also contributed to the development of the professional writer. Film, radio, and television are sources of entertainment, information, and education that provide employment

QUICK FACTS

School Subjects
Earth science
English

Personal Skills
Communication/ideas
Technical/scientific

Work Environment
Indoors and outdoors
Primarily multiple locations

Minimum Education Level
Bachelor's degree

Salary Range
$24,320 to $46,420 to
$89,940+

Certification or Licensing
Voluntary

Outlook
About as fast as the average

DOT
131

GOE
01.02.01

NOC
5121

O*NET-SOC
27-3042.00, 27-3043.00

for thousands of writers. Today, the computer industry and Internet Web sites have also created the need for more writers.

As our world becomes more complex and people seek even more information, professional writers have become increasingly important. And, as science takes giant steps forward and discoveries are made every day that impact our lives, skilled science writers are needed to document these changes and disseminate the information to the general public and more specialized audiences.

THE JOB

Science writers usually write for the general public. They translate scientific information into articles and reports that the general public and the media can understand. They might write about global warming and its effects on coastal communities, the cancer-fighting properties of a newly discovered tropical plant, efforts by scientists to fight the spread of avian flu, a new species of dinosaur discovered in the Saharan desert, efforts by the federal government to force chemical manufacturers to comply with air and water pollution regulations, and countless other topics. Good writers who cover the subjects thoroughly have inquisitive minds and enjoy looking for additional information that might add to their articles. They research the topic to gain a thorough understanding of the subject matter. This may require hours of research on the Internet, or in corporate, university, or public libraries. Writers always need good background information regarding a subject before they can write about it.

In order to get the information required, writers may interview professionals such as scientists, engineers, managers, and others who are familiar with the subject. Writers must know how to present the information so it can be understood. This requires knowing the audience and how to reach them. For example, an article on tsunamis may need graphs, photos, or historical facts. Writers sometimes enlist the help of technical illustrators or engineers in order to add a visual dimension to their work.

For example, if reporting on a tsunami that has killed thousands of people in the Pacific, writers will need to illustrate the factors that cause a tsunami (earthquakes, but also underwater landslides, volcanic eruptions, and even very rarely the impact of a large meteorite in the ocean). The public will also want to know what areas of the earth are affected by tsunamis (coastal areas), what the warning signs are (a recent earthquake in the region, suddenly receding waters from coastal areas, etc.), and what governments are doing

Earth Science Magazines on the Web

American Journal of Botany
http://www.botany.org/publications

BioScience
http://www.aibs.org/bioscience

CaGIS Journal
http://www.cartogis.org/publications

Crops and Soils
https://www.soils.org/publications.html

Ecology
http://esa.org/publications

Fossil News: Journal of Avocational Paleontology
http://www.fossilnews.com

Geotimes
http://www.geotimes.org/current

Journal of the Atmospheric Sciences
http://www.ametsoc.org/pubs/journals/index.html

Limnology and Oceanography
http://www.aslo.org/lo

Mineralogical Record
http://www.minrec.org

National Geographic
http://www.nationalgeographic.com

Ocean
http://www.oceanmag.org

Plant Science Bulletin
http://www.botany.org/publications

The Professional Geographer
http://www.aag.org/Publications/pgweb1.html

Rangeland Ecology & Management
http://www.srmjournals.org

Rangelands
http://www.srmjournals.org

to prepare their citizens for tsunamis (educating the public about warning signs of tsunamis, creating early warning networks among tsunami-threatened nations, etc.). In addition, interviews with scientists and tsunami survivors add a personal touch to the story.

Writers usually need to work quickly because news-related stories are often deadline-oriented. Because science can be so complex, science writers also need to help the audience understand and evaluate the information. Writing for the Web encompasses most journalistic guidelines including time constraints and sometimes space constraints.

Some science writers specialize in their subject matter. For instance, a science writer may write only about volcanoes and earn a reputation as the best writer in that subject area. Or they may limit their writing or research to environmental science subjects, or may be even more specific and focus only on air pollution issues.

"This career can have various appeals," says Barbara Gastel, M.D., coordinator of the master of science program in science and technology journalism at Texas A&M University. "People can combine their interest in science or medicine with their love of writing. It is a good field for a generalist who likes science and doesn't want to be tied to research in one area. Plus," she adds, "it is always fun to get things published."

Some writers may choose to be freelance writers either on a full- or part-time basis, or to supplement other jobs. Freelance science writers are self-employed writers who work with small and large companies, research institutions, or publishing firms on a contract or hourly basis. They may specialize in writing about a specific scientific subject for one or two clients, or they may write about a broad range of subjects for a number of different clients. Many freelance writers write articles, papers, or reports and then attempt to get them published in newspapers, trade, or consumer publications.

REQUIREMENTS

High School

If you are considering a career as a writer, you should take English, journalism, and communication courses in high school. Computer classes will also be helpful. If you know in high school that you want to do scientific writing, it would be to your advantage to take biology, physiology, earth science, chemistry, physics, math, and other science-related courses. If your school offers journalism courses and you have the chance to work on the school newspaper or yearbook, you should take advantage of these opportunities. Part-time employment at newspapers, publishing companies, or scientific research facilities can also provide experience and insight regarding this career.

Postsecondary Training

Although not all writers are college-educated, today's jobs almost always require a bachelor's degree. Many writers earn an undergraduate degree in English, journalism, or liberal arts and then obtain a master's degree in a communications field such as writing. A good liberal arts education is important since you are often required to write about many subject areas. Science-related courses (or even pursuing a science-related field as a second major) are highly recommended. You should investigate internship programs that give you experience in the communications department of a corporation, engineering firm, or research facility. Some newspapers, magazines, or public relations firms also have internships that give you the opportunity to write.

Some people find that after working as a writer, their interests are strong in science and they evolve into that writing specialty. They may return to school and enter a master's degree program or take some additional courses related specifically to science writing. Similarly, science majors may find that they like the writing aspect of their jobs and return to school to pursue a career as a science writer.

Other Requirements

If you are considering a career as a science writer, you should enjoy writing, be able to write well, and be able to express your ideas and those of others clearly. You should have an excellent knowledge of the English language and have superb grammar and spelling skills. You should be skilled in research techniques and be computer literate and familiar with software programs related to writing and publishing. You should be curious, enjoy learning about new things, and have an interest in science. You need to be detail-oriented since many of your writing assignments will require that you obtain and relay accurate and detailed information. Interpersonal skills are also important because many jobs require that you interact with and interview professional people such as scientists, engineers, and researchers. You must be able to meet deadlines and work under pressure.

EXPLORING

As a high school or college student, you can test your interest and aptitude in the field of writing by serving as a reporter or writer on school newspapers, yearbooks, and literary magazines. Attending writing workshops and taking writing classes will give you the opportunity to practice and sharpen your skills.

Community newspapers often welcome contributions from outside sources, although they may not have the resources to pay for them. Jobs in bookstores, magazine shops, libraries, and even newsstands offer a chance to become familiar with various publications. If you are interested in science writing, try to get a part-time job in a research laboratory, interview science writers, and read good science writing in major newspapers such as the *New York Times* or the *Wall Street Journal* or in publications produced by major science associations.

Information on writing as a career may also be obtained by visiting local newspapers and publishing houses and interviewing some of the writers who work there. Career conferences and other guidance programs frequently include speakers from local or national organizations who can provide information on communication careers.

Some professional organizations such as the Society for Technical Communication welcome students as members and have special student membership rates and career information. In addition, participation in professional organizations gives you the opportunity to meet and visit with people in this career field.

EMPLOYERS

Many science writers are employed, often on a freelance basis, by newspaper, magazine, and book publishers, and the broadcast industries as well. Internet publishing is a growing field that hires science writers. Science writers are also employed by scientific research companies; government research facilities; federal, state, and local agencies; manufacturing companies; research and development departments of corporations; and the chemical industries. Large colleges and universities often employ science writers.

STARTING OUT

A fair amount of experience is required to gain a high-level position in this field. Most writers start out in entry-level positions. These jobs may be listed with college career services offices, or you may apply directly to the human resources departments of publishing companies, corporations, institutions, universities, research facilities, nonprofit organizations, and government facilities that hire science writers. Many firms now hire writers directly upon application or recommendation of college professors and career services offices. Want ads in newspapers and trade journals are another source for jobs. Serving an internship in college can give you the advantage of knowing people who can give you personal recommendations.

Internships are also excellent ways to build your portfolio. Employers in the communications field are usually interested in seeing samples of your published writing assembled in an organized portfolio or scrapbook. Working on your college's magazine or newspaper staff can help you build a portfolio. Sometimes small, regional or local magazines and newspapers will also buy articles or assign short pieces for you to write. You should attempt to build your portfolio with good writing samples. Be sure to include the type of writing you are interested in doing, if possible.

You may need to begin your career as a junior writer or editor and work your way up. This usually involves library research, preparation of rough drafts for part or all of a report, cataloging, and other related writing tasks. These are generally carried on under the supervision of a senior writer.

Many science writers enter the field after working in public relations departments or science-related industries. They may use their skills to transfer to specialized writing positions or they may take additional courses or graduate work that focuses on writing or documentation skills.

ADVANCEMENT

Writers with only an undergraduate degree may choose to earn a graduate degree in science writing, corporate communications, document design, or a related program. An advanced degree may open doors to more progressive career options.

Many experienced science writers are often promoted to head writing, documentation, or public relations departments within corporations or institutions. Some may become recognized experts in their field and their writings may be in demand by trade journals, newspapers, magazines, and the broadcast industry. Writers employed by newspapers and magazines may advance by working for larger, more prestigious publications.

As freelance writers prove themselves and work successfully with clients, they may be able to demand increased contract fees or hourly rates.

EARNINGS

Although there are no specific salary studies for science writers, salary information for all writers is available. The U.S. Department of Labor reports that the median annual salary for writers in 2005 was $46,420. Salaries ranged from less than $24,320 to more than $89,940. Mean annual earnings for writers employed by newspaper, book, and directory publishers were $47,950 in 2005.

According to the Society for Technical Communication, the median salary for technical writers and editors in the United States was $60,240 in 2006. The U.S. Department of Labor reports that salaries for technical writers ranged from less than $33,250 to more than $87,550 in 2005.

Freelance writers' earnings can vary depending on their expertise, reputation, and the articles they are contracted to write.

Most full-time writing positions offer the usual benefits such as insurance, sick leave, and paid vacation. Some jobs also provide tuition reimbursement and retirement benefits. Freelance writers must pay for their own insurance. However, there are professional associations that may offer group insurance rates for its members.

WORK ENVIRONMENT

Work environment depends on the type of science writing and the employer. Generally, writers work in an office or research environment. Writers for the news media sometimes work in noisy surroundings. Some writers travel to research information and conduct interviews while other employers may confine research to local libraries or the Internet. In addition, some employers require writers to conduct research interviews over the phone, rather than in person.

Although the workweek usually runs 35 to 40 hours in a normal office setting, many writers may have to work overtime to cover a story, interview people, meet deadlines, or to disseminate information in a timely manner. The newspaper and broadcasting industries deliver the news 24 hours a day, seven days a week. Writers often work nights and weekends to meet press deadlines or to cover a late-developing story.

Each day may bring new and interesting situations. Some stories may even take writers to remote and exotic locales. Other assignments may be boring or they may take place in less than desirable settings, where interview subjects may be rude, busy, and unwilling to talk or conditions may be cold, snowy, rainy, or otherwise uncomfortable. One of the most difficult elements for writers may be meeting deadlines or gathering information. People who are the most content as writers work well with deadline pressure.

OUTLOOK

According to the U.S. Department of Labor, there is strong competition for writing and editing jobs, and growth in writing careers should occur at an average rate through 2014. Opportunities will be very good for science writers, as continued developments in the field will drive the need for skilled writers to put complex scientific information in terms that a wide and varied audience can understand.

FOR MORE INFORMATION

To read advice for beginning science writers, visit the NASW Web site.
   National Association of Science Writers (NASW)
   PO Box 890
   Hedgesville, WV 25427-0890
   Tel: 304-754-5077
   http://www.nasw.org

For information on scholarships and student memberships aimed at those preparing for a career in technical communication, contact
   Society for Technical Communication
   901 North Stuart Street, Suite 904
   Arlington, VA 22203-1822
   Tel: 703-522-4114
   Email: stc@stc.org
   http://www.stc.org

Soil Conservationists and Technicians

OVERVIEW

Soil conservationists develop conservation plans to help farmers and ranchers, developers, homeowners, and government officials best use their land while adhering to government conservation regulations. They suggest plans to conserve and reclaim soil, preserve or restore wetlands and other rare ecological areas, rotate crops for increased yields and soil conservation, reduce water pollution, and restore or increase wildlife populations. They assess land users' needs, costs, maintenance requirements, and the life expectancy of various conservation practices. They plan design specifications using survey and field information, technical guides, and engineering field manuals. Soil conservationists also give talks to various organizations to educate land users and the public about how to conserve and restore soil and water resources. Many of their recommendations are based on information provided to them by *soil scientists*.

Soil conservation technicians work more directly with land users by putting the ideas and plans of the conservationist into action. In their work they use basic engineering and surveying tools, instruments, and techniques. They perform engineering surveys and design and implement conservation practices like terraces and grassed waterways. Soil conservation technicians monitor projects during and after construction and periodically revisit the site to evaluate the practices and plans.

HISTORY

In 1908, President Theodore Roosevelt appointed a National Conservation Commission to oversee the proper conservation of the country's natural resources. As a result, many state and local conservation organizations were formed, and Americans began to take a serious interest in preserving their land's natural resources.

Despite this interest, however, conservation methods were not always understood or implemented. For example, farmers in the southern Great Plains, wanting to harvest a cash crop, planted many thousands of acres of wheat during the early decades of the 20th century. The crop was repeated year after year until the natural grasslands of the area were destroyed and the soil was depleted of nutrients. When the area experienced prolonged droughts combined with the naturally occurring high winds, devastating dust storms swept the land during the 1930s. Parts of Oklahoma, Texas, Kansas, New Mexico, and Colorado suffered from severe soil erosion that resulted in desert-like conditions, and this ruined area became known as the Dust Bowl.

As a result of what happened to the Dust Bowl, Congress established the Natural Resources Conservation Service of the U.S. Department of Agriculture in 1935. Because more than 800 million tons of topsoil had already been blown away by the winds over the plains, the job of reclaiming the land through wise conservation practices was not an easy one. In addition to the large areas of the Great Plains that had become desert land, there were other badly eroded lands throughout the country.

Fortunately, emergency planning came to the aid of the newly established conservation program. The Civilian Conservation Corps (CCC) was created to help alleviate unemployment during the Great Depression of the 1930s. The CCC established camps in rural areas and assigned people to aid in many different kinds of conservation. Soil conservationists directed those portions of the CCC program designed to halt the loss of topsoil by wind and water action.

Much progress has been made in the years since the Natural Resources Conservation Service was established. Wasted land has been reclaimed and further loss has been prevented. Land-grant colleges have initiated programs to help farmers understand the principles and procedures of soil conservation. The Cooperative Research, Education, and Extension Service (within the Department of Agriculture) provides workers who are skilled in soil conservation to work with these programs.

A soil conservation technician examines a soil sample. *(Scott Bauer/ Agricultural Research Service/U.S. Department of Agriculture)*

Throughout the United States today there are several thousand federally appointed soil conservation districts. A worker employed by the government works in these districts to demonstrate soil conservation to farmers and agricultural businesses. There are usually one or more professional soil conservationists and one or more soil conservation technicians working in each district.

THE JOB

Soil sustains plant and animal life, influences water and air quality, and supports human health and habitation. Its quality has a major impact on ecological balance, biological diversity, air quality, water flow, and plant growth, including crops and forestation. Soil conservationists and technicians help scientists and engineers collect samples and data to determine soil quality, identify problems, and develop plans to better manage the land. They work with farmers, agricultural professionals, landowners, range managers, and public and private agencies to establish and maintain sound conservation practices.

A farmer or landowner contacts soil conservationists to help identify soil quality problems, improve soil quality, maintain it, or stop or reverse soil degradation. Conservationists visit the site to gather information, beginning with past and current uses of the soil and future plans for the site. They consult precipitation and soil maps and try to determine if the way land is being currently used is somehow degrading the soil quality. Conservationists consider irrigation practices, fertilizer use, and tillage systems. At least a five- to 10-year history of land use is most helpful for working in this field.

Site observation reveals signs of soil quality problems. The farmer or landowner can point out areas of concern that occur regularly, such as wet spots, salt accumulation, rills and gullies, or excessive runoff water that could indicate erosion, stunted plant growth, or low crop yield. Samples are taken from these areas and tested for such physical, chemical, and biological properties as soil fertility, soil structure, soil stability, water storage and availability, and nutrient retention. Conservationists also look at plant characteristics, such as rooting depth, which can indicate density or compaction of the soil.

Once all the data are gathered and samples tested, conservationists analyze the results. They look for patterns and trends. If necessary, they take additional samples to verify discrepancies or confirm results. They prepare a report for the farmer or landowner.

A team of conservationists, engineers, scientists, and the landowners propose alternative solutions for soil problems. All the alternatives must be weighed carefully for their possible effects on ecological balance, natural resources, economic factors, and social or cultural factors. The landowner makes the final decision on which solutions to use and a plan is drafted.

After the plan is in place, soil conservationists and technicians continue to monitor and evaluate soil conditions, usually over a period of several years. Periodic soil sampling shows whether progress is being made, and if not, changes can be made to the plan.

These brief examples show how the process works. A farmer has a problem with crop disease. He sees that the yield is reduced and the health of plants is poor. Soil conservationists and technicians consider possible causes and test soil for pests, nutrient deficiencies, lack of biological diversity, saturated soil, and compacted layers. Depending on test results, conservationists might suggest a pest-management program, an improved drainage system, the use of animal manure, or crop rotation.

Another farmer notices the formation of rills and gullies on his land along with a thinning topsoil layer. Soil conservationists' research shows that the erosion is due to such factors as lack of cover, excessive tillage that moves soil down a slope, intensive crop rotation, and low organic matter. Suggested solutions include reducing tillage, using animal manure, planting cover crops or strip crops, and using windbreaks.

Conservationists and technicians who work for the Bureau of Land Management, which oversees hundreds of millions of acres of public domain, help survey publicly owned areas and pinpoint land features to determine the best use of public lands. Soil conservation technicians in the Bureau of Reclamation assist civil, construction, materials, or general engineers. Their job is to oversee certain phases of such projects as the construction of dams and irrigation planning. The bureau's ultimate goal is the control of water and soil resources for the benefit of farms, homes, and cities.

Other soil conservationists and technicians work as *range technicians*, who help determine the value of rangeland, its grazing capabilities, erosion hazards, and livestock potential. *Physical science technicians* gather data in the field, studying the physical characteristics of the soil, make routine chemical analyses, and set up and operate test apparatus. *Cartographic survey technicians* work with *cartographers* (mapmakers) to map or chart the earth or graphically represent geographical information, survey the public domain, set boundaries, pinpoint land features, and determine the most beneficial public use. *Engineering technicians* conduct field tests and oversee some phases of construction on dams and irrigation projects. They also measure acreage, place property boundaries, and define drainage areas on maps. *Surveying technicians* perform surveys for field measurement and mapping, to plan for construction, to check the accuracy of dredging operations, or to provide reference points and lines for related work. They gather data for the design and construction of highways, dams, topographic maps, and nautical or aeronautical charts.

REQUIREMENTS

High School

While in high school, you should take at least one year each of algebra, geometry, and trigonometry. Take several years of English to develop your writing, research, and speaking skills as these are skills you will need when compiling reports and working with others. Science classes, of course, are important to take, including earth science, biology, and chemistry. If your high school offers agriculture classes, be sure to take any relating to land use, crop production, and soils.

Postsecondary Training

Conservationists hold bachelor's degrees in areas such as general agriculture, range management, crop or soil science, forestry, and agricultural engineering. Teaching and research positions require further graduate level education in a natural resources field. Though government jobs do not necessarily require a college degree (a combination of appropriate experience and education can serve as substitute), a college education can make you more desirable for a position.

Typical beginning courses include applied mathematics, communication skills, basic soils, botany, chemistry, zoology, and introduction to range management. Advanced courses include American government, surveying, forestry, game management, soil and water conservation, economics, fish management, and conservation engineering.

Conservationists and technicians must have some practical experience in the use of soil conservation techniques before they enter the field. Many schools require students to work in the field during the school year or during summer vacation before they can be awarded their degree. Jobs are available in the federal park systems and with privately owned industries.

Certification or Licensing

No certification or license is required of soil conservationists and technicians; however, becoming certified can improve your skills and professional standing. The American Society of Agronomy offers voluntary certification in soil science/classification.

Most government agencies require applicants to take a competitive examination for consideration.

Other Requirements

Soil conservationists and technicians must be able to apply practical as well as theoretical knowledge to their work. You must have a working knowledge of soil and water characteristics; be skilled in management of woodlands, wildlife areas, and recreation areas; and have knowledge of surveying instruments and practices, mapping, and the procedures used for interpreting aerial photographs.

Soil conservationists and technicians should also be able to write clear, concise reports to demonstrate and explain the results of tests, studies, and recommendations. A love for the outdoors and an appreciation for all natural resources are essential for success and personal fulfillment in this job.

EXPLORING

One of the best ways to become acquainted with soil conservation work and technology is through summer or part-time work on a farm or at a natural park. Other ways to explore this career include joining a local chapter of the 4-H Club or National FFA Organization (formerly Future Farmers of America). Science courses that include lab sections and mathematics courses focusing on practical problem solving will also help give you a feel for this kind of work.

EMPLOYERS

Nearly two-thirds of all conservation workers are employed by local and federal government agencies. At the federal level, most soil conservationists and technicians work for the Natural Resources Conservation Service, the Bureau of Land Management, and the Bureau of Reclamation. Others work for agencies at the state and county level. Soil conservationists and technicians also work for private agencies and firms such as banks and loan agencies, mining or steel companies, and public utilities. A small percentage of workers are self-employed consultants who advise private industry owners and government agencies.

STARTING OUT

Most students gain outside experience by working a summer job in their area of interest. You can get information on summer positions through your school's career services office. Often, contacts made on summer jobs lead to permanent employment after graduation.

College career counselors and faculty members are often valuable sources of advice and information on finding employment.

Most soil conservationists and technicians find work with state, county, or federal agencies. Hiring procedures for these jobs vary according to the level of government in which the applicant is seeking work. In general, however, students begin the application procedure during the fourth semester of their program and take some form of competitive examination as part of the process. College career services personnel can help students find out about the application procedures. Representatives of government agencies often visit college campuses to explain employment opportunities to students and sometimes to recruit for their agencies.

ADVANCEMENT

Soil conservationists and technicians usually start out with a local conservation district to gain experience and expertise before advancing to the state, regional, or national level.

In many cases, conservationists and technicians continue their education while working by taking evening courses at a local college or technical institute. Federal agencies that employ conservationists and technicians have a policy of promotion from within. Because of this policy, there is a continuing opportunity for such workers to advance through the ranks. The degree of advancement that all conservationists and technicians can expect in their working careers is determined by their aptitudes, abilities, and, of course, their desire to advance.

Workers seeking a more dramatic change can transfer their skills to related jobs outside the conservation industry, such as farming or land appraisal.

EARNINGS

The majority of soil conservationists and technicians work for the federal government, and their salaries are determined by their government service rating. In 2005, the average annual salary for soil conservationists employed by the federal government was $60,671, according to the *Occupational Outlook Handbook*. Starting salaries for those with bachelor's degrees employed by the federal government was $24,677 or $30,567 in 2005, depending on academic achievement. Those with master's degrees earned a higher starting salary of $37,390 or $45,239, and with a doctorate, $54,221.

The U.S. Department of Labor reports that median earnings for conservation scientists were $53,350 in 2005. Some conservation scientists earned less than $30,730, while others earned $81,910 or more annually.

The U.S. Department of Labor reports that median earnings for forest and conservation technicians (including those who specialize in soil science) were $28,540 in 2005. Salaries ranged from less than $20,450 to more than $45,700 annually.

The salaries of conservationists and technicians working for private firms or agencies are roughly comparable to those paid by the federal government. Earnings at the state and local levels vary depending on the region but are typically lower.

Government jobs and larger private industries offer comprehensive benefit packages that are usually more generous than those offered at smaller firms.

WORK ENVIRONMENT

Soil conservationists and technicians usually work 40 hours per week except in unusual or emergency situations. They have opportunities to travel, especially when they work for federal agencies.

Soil conservation is an outdoor job. Workers travel to work sites by car but must often walk great distances to an assigned area. Although they sometimes work from aerial photographs and other on-site pictures, they cannot work from pictures alone. They must visit the spot that presents the problem in order to make appropriate recommendations.

Although soil conservationists and technicians spend much of their working time outdoors, indoor work is also necessary when generating detailed reports of their work to agency offices.

In their role as assistants to professionals, soil conservation technicians often assume the role of government public relations representatives when dealing with landowners and land managers. They must be able to explain the underlying principles of the structures that they design and the surveys that they perform.

To meet these and other requirements of the job, conservationists and technicians should be prepared to continue their education both formally and informally throughout their careers. They must stay aware of current periodicals and studies so that they can keep up-to-date in their areas of specialization.

Soil conservationists and technicians gain satisfaction from knowing that their work is vitally important to the nation's economy and environment. Without their expertise, large portions of land in the United States could become barren within a generation.

OUTLOOK

The U.S. Department of Labor predicts employment for conservation scientists (a category including soil conservationists) will grow slower than the average for all occupations through 2014, mainly due to decreased federal spending in this area. Nevertheless, the need for government involvement in protecting natural resources should remain strong. More opportunities may be available with state and local government agencies, which are aware of needs in their areas. The vast majority of America's cropland has suffered from some sort of erosion, and only continued efforts by soil conservation professionals can prevent a dangerous depletion of our most valuable resource: fertile soil.

Some soil conservationists and technicians are employed as research and testing experts for public utility companies, banks and loan agencies, and mining or steel companies. At present, a relatively small number of soil conservation workers are employed by these firms or agencies. However, it is these private-sector areas that will provide the most employment opportunities over the next 10 years.

FOR MORE INFORMATION

For information on soil conservation careers and certification, contact
American Society of Agronomy
677 South Segoe Road
Madison, WI 53711-1086
Tel: 608-273-8080
Email: headquarters@agronomy.org
http://www.agronomy.org

For information on seminars, issues affecting soil scientists, and educational institutions offering soil science programs, contact
National Society of Consulting Soil Scientists
PO Box 724
Sandpoint, ID 83864-0724
Tel: 800-535-7148
Email: info2007@nscss.com
http://www.nscss.org

Contact the NRCS for information on government soil conservation careers. Its Web site has information on volunteer opportunities.

Natural Resources Conservation Service (NRCS)
U.S. Department of Agriculture
Attn: Legislative and Public Affairs Division
PO Box 2890
Washington, DC 20013-2890
http://www.nrcs.usda.gov

For information on soil conservation, college student chapters, and publications, contact
Soil and Water Conservation Society
945 SW Ankeny Road
Ankeny, IA 50023-9723
Tel: 515-289-2331
http://www.swcs.org

For the career brochure Soils Sustain Life, *contact*
Soil Science Society of America
677 South Segoe Road
Madison, WI 53711-1086
Tel: 608-273-8080
http://www.soils.org

Soil Scientists

OVERVIEW

Soil scientists study the physical, chemical, and biological characteristics of soils to determine the most productive and effective planting strategies. Their research aids in producing larger, healthier crops and more environmentally sound farming procedures. There are about 17,000 soil and plant scientists employed in the United States.

HISTORY

Hundreds of years ago, farmers planted crops without restriction; they were unaware that soil could be depleted of necessary nutrients by overuse. When crops were poor, farmers often blamed the weather instead of their farming techniques.

Soil, one of our most important natural resources, was taken for granted until its condition became too bad to ignore. An increasing population, moreover, made the United States aware that its own welfare depends on fertile soil capable of producing food for hundreds of millions of people.

Increasing concerns about feeding a growing nation brought agricultural practices into reevaluation. In 1862, the U.S. Department of Agriculture (USDA) was created to give farmers information about new crops and improved farming techniques. Although the department started small, today the USDA is one of the largest agencies of the federal government.

Following the creation of the USDA, laws were created to further promote and protect farmers. The 1933 Agricultural Adjustment Act inaugurated a policy of giving direct government aid to farmers. Two years later, the Natural Resources Conservation Service developed

A soil scientist (left) and a technician section a core sample from a conventionally tilled cornfield in preparation for determining total carbon with soil depth. *(Peggy Greb/Agricultural Research Service/U.S. Department of Agriculture)*

after disastrous dust storms blew away millions of tons of valuable topsoil and destroyed fertile cropland throughout the midwestern states.

Since 1937, states have organized themselves into soil conservation districts. Each local division coordinates with the USDA, assigning soil scientists and soil conservationists to help local farmers establish and maintain farming practices that will use land in the wisest possible ways.

THE JOB

Soil is formed by the breaking of rocks and the decay of trees, plants, and animals. It may take as long as 500 years to make just one inch of topsoil. Unwise and wasteful farming methods can destroy that inch of soil in just a few short years. In addition, rainstorms may carry thousands of pounds of precious topsoil away and dissolve chemicals that are necessary to grow healthy crops through a process called erosion. Soil scientists work with engineers to address these issues.

Soil scientists spend much of their time outdoors, investigating fields, advising farmers about crop rotation or fertilizers, assessing field drainage, and taking soil samples. After researching an area, they may suggest certain crops to farmers to protect bare earth from the ravages of the wind and weather.

Soil scientists may also specialize in one particular aspect of the work. For example, they may work as a *soil mapper* or *soil surveyor*. These specialists study soil structure, origins, and capabilities through field observations, laboratory examinations, and controlled experimentation. Their investigations are aimed at determining the most suitable uses for a particular soil.

Soil fertility experts develop practices that will increase or maintain crop size. They must consider both the type of soil and the crop planted in their analysis. Various soils react differently when exposed to fertilizers, soil additives, crop rotation, and other farming techniques.

All soil scientists work in laboratories. They examine soil samples under the microscope to determine bacterial and plant-food components. They also write reports based on their field notes and analyses done within the lab.

Soil science is part of the science of agronomy, which encompasses crop science. Soil and crop scientists work together in agricultural experiment stations during all seasons, doing research on crop production, soil fertility, and various kinds of soil management.

Some soil and crop scientists travel to remote sections of the world in search of plants and grasses that may thrive in this country and contribute to our food supply, pasture land, or soil replenishing efforts. Some scientists go overseas to advise farmers in other countries on how to treat their soils. Those with advanced degrees can teach college agriculture courses and conduct research projects.

REQUIREMENTS

High School

If you're interested in pursuing a career in agronomy, you should take college preparatory courses covering subjects such as math, science, English, and public speaking. Science courses, such as earth science, biology, and chemistry, are particularly important. Since much of your future work will involve calculations, you should take four years of high school math. You can learn a lot about farming methods and conditions by taking agriculture classes if your high school offers them. Computer science courses are also a good choice to familiarize yourself with this technology. You should also take English and speech courses, since soil scientists must write reports and make presentations about their findings.

Postsecondary Training

A bachelor's degree in agriculture or soil science is the minimum educational requirement to become a soil scientist. Typical courses include physics, geology, bacteriology, botany, chemistry, soil and plant morphology, soil fertility, soil classification, and soil genesis.

Research and teaching positions usually require higher levels of education. Most colleges of agriculture also offer master's and doctoral degrees. In addition to studying agriculture or soil science, students can specialize in biology, chemistry, physics, or engineering.

Certification or Licensing

Though not required, many soil scientists may seek certification to enhance their careers. The American Society of Agronomy offers certification programs in the following areas: crop advisory, agronomy, and soil science/classification. In order to be accepted into a program, applicants must meet certain levels of education and experience.

Other Requirements

Soil scientists must be able to work effectively both on their own and with others on projects, either outdoors or in the lab. Technology is increasingly used in this profession; an understanding of word processing, the Internet, multimedia software, databases, and even computer programming can be useful. Soil scientists spend many hours outdoors in all kinds of weather, so they must be able to endure sometimes difficult and uncomfortable physical conditions. They must be detail-oriented to do accurate research, and they should enjoy solving puzzles—figuring out, for example, why a crop isn't flourishing and what fertilizers should be used.

EXPLORING

The National FFA Organization can introduce you to the concerns of farmers and researchers. A 4-H club can also give you valuable experience in agriculture. Contact the local branch of these organizations, your county's soil conservation department, or other government agencies to learn about regional projects. If you live in an agricultural community, you may be able to find opportunities for part-time or summer work on a farm or ranch.

EMPLOYERS

Most soil scientists work for state or federal departments of agriculture. However, they may also work for other public employers, such as land appraisal boards, land-grant colleges and universities, and conservation departments. Soil scientists who work overseas may be employed by the U.S. Agency for International Development.

Soil scientists are needed in private industries as well, such as agricultural service companies, banks, insurance and real estate firms, food products companies, wholesale distributors, and environmental and engineering consulting groups. Private firms may hire soil scientists for sales or research positions. Approximately 17,000 soil and plant scientists are employed in the United States.

STARTING OUT

In the public sector, college graduates can apply directly to the Natural Resources Conservation Service of the Department of Agriculture, the Department of the Interior, the Environmental Protection Agency, or other state government agencies for beginning positions. University placement services generally have listings for these openings as well as opportunities available in private industry.

ADVANCEMENT

Salary increases are the most common form of advancement for soil scientists. The nature of the job may not change appreciably even after many years of service. Higher administrative and supervisory positions are few in comparison with the number of jobs that must be done in the field.

Opportunities for advancement will be higher for those with advanced degrees. For soil scientists engaged in teaching, advancement may translate into a higher academic rank with more responsibility. In private business firms, soil scientists have opportunities to advance into positions such as department head or research director. Supervisory and manager positions are also available in state agencies such as road or conservation departments.

EARNINGS

According to the U.S. Department of Labor, median earnings in 2005 for soil and plant scientists were $54,530. The lowest paid 10 percent earned less than $32,360; the middle 50 percent earned between $40,590 and $70,830; and the highest paid 10 percent made more than $91,520.

Federal salaries for soil scientists were higher; in 2005, they made an average of $70,200 a year. Government earnings depend in large part on levels of experience and education. Those with doctorates and a great deal of experience may be qualified for higher government positions, with salaries ranging from $80,000 to $100,000. Other than short-term research projects, most jobs offer health and retirement benefits in addition to an annual salary.

WORK ENVIRONMENT

Most soil scientists work 40 hours a week. Their job is varied, ranging from fieldwork collecting samples, to lab work analyzing their findings. Some jobs may involve travel, even to foreign countries. Other positions may include teaching or supervisory responsibilities for field training programs.

OUTLOOK

The *Occupational Outlook Handbook* reports that employment within the field of soil science is expected to grow more slowly than the average for all occupations through 2014. The career of soil scientist is affected by the government's involvement in farming studies; as a result, budget cuts at the federal and (especially) state levels will limit funding for this type of job. However, private businesses will continue to demand soil scientists for research and sales positions. Companies dealing with seed, fertilizers, or farm equipment are examples of private industries that hire soil scientists.

Technological advances in equipment and methods of conservation will allow scientists to better protect the environment, as well as improve farm production. Scientists' ability to evaluate soils and plants will improve with more precise research methods. Combine-mounted yield monitors will produce data as the farmer crosses the field, and satellites will provide more detailed field information. With computer images, scientists will also be able to examine plant roots more carefully.

A continued challenge facing future soil scientists will be convincing farmers to change their current methods of tilling and chemical treatment in favor of environmentally safer methods. They must encourage farmers to balance increased agricultural output with the protection of our limited natural resources.

FOR MORE INFORMATION

The ASA has information on careers, certification, and college chapters. For details, contact

American Society of Agronomy (ASA)
677 South Segoe Road
Madison, WI 53711-1086
Tel: 608-273-8080
Email: headquarters@agronomy.org
http://www.agronomy.org

Contact the NRCS for information on government soil conservation careers. Its Web site features information on volunteer opportunities.
Natural Resources Conservation Service (NRCS)
U.S. Department of Agriculture
Attn: Legislative and Public Affairs Division
PO Box 2890
Washington, DC 20013-2890
http://www.nrcs.usda.gov

For information on seminars, issues affecting soil scientists, and educational institutions offering soil science programs, contact
National Society of Consulting Soil Scientists
PO Box 724
Sandpoint, ID 83864-0724
Tel: 800-535-7148
Email: info2007@nscss.com
http://www.nscss.org

For information on soil conservation, college student chapters, and publications, contact
Soil and Water Conservation Society
945 SW Ankeny Road
Ankeny, IA 50023-9723
Tel: 515-289-2331
http://www.swcs.org

For the career brochure Soils Sustain Life, *contact*
Soil Science Society of America
677 South Segoe Road
Madison, WI 53711-1086
Tel: 608-273-8080
http://www.soils.org

Surveying and Mapping Technicians

QUICK FACTS

School Subjects
Geography
Mathematics

Personal Skills
Following instructions
Technical/scientific

Work Environment
Primarily outdoors
Primarily multiple locations

Minimum Education Level
Some postsecondary training

Salary Range
$19,300 to $31,290 to
$52,000+

Certification or Licensing
Voluntary

Outlook
About as fast as the average

DOT
018

GOE
02.08.01

NOC
2254

O*NET-SOC
17-3031.00, 17-3031.01,
17-3031.02

OVERVIEW

Surveying and mapping technicians help determine, describe, and record geographic areas or features. They are usually the leading assistant to the professional surveyor, civil engineer, and mapmaker. They operate modern surveying and mapping instruments and may participate in other operations. Technicians must have a basic knowledge of the current practices and legal implications of surveys to establish and record property size, shape, topography, and boundaries. They often supervise other assistants during routine surveying conducted within the bounds established by a professional surveyor. There are approximately 65,000 surveying and mapping technicians working in the United States.

HISTORY

From ancient times, people have needed to define their property boundaries. Marking established areas of individual or group ownership was a basis for the development of early civilizations. Landholding became important in ancient Egypt, and with the development of hieroglyphics, people were able to keep a record of their holdings. Eventually, nations found it necessary not only to mark property boundaries but also to record principal routes of commerce and transportation. For example, records of the Babylonians tell of their canals and irrigation ditches. The Romans surveyed and mapped their empire's principal roads. In the early days of colonial exploration, surveyors and their technical helpers were among the first and most-needed workers. They established new land ownership by surveying and filing claims. Since then, precise and accurate geographical measurements have been needed to determine the location of a highway, the site of a building, the right-of-way for drainage ditches, telephone, and power lines, and for the charting of unexplored land, bodies of water, and underground mines.

Early surveying processes required at least two people. A technical scientist served as the leader, or professional surveyor. This scientist was assisted by helpers to make measurements with chains, tapes, and wheel rotations, where each rotation accounted for a known length of distance. The helpers held rods marked for location purposes and placed other markers to define important points.

As measuring instruments have become more complex, the speed, scope, and accuracy of surveying have improved. Developments in surveying and mapping technology have made great changes in the planning and construction of highway systems and structures of all kinds. For roadway route selection and design, technicians increasingly use photogrammetry, which uses plotting machines to scribe routes from aerial photographs of rural or urban areas. Route data obtained by photogrammetry may then be processed through computers to calculate land acquisition, grading, and construction costs. Photogrammetry is faster and far more accurate than former methods. In addition, new electronic distance-measuring devices have brought surveying to a higher level of precision. Technicians can measure distance more quickly, accurately, and economically than was possible with tapes, rods, and chains.

In addition to photogrammetry, the use of computers in data processing has extended surveying and mapping careers past the earth's surface. Technicians now help to make detailed maps of ocean floors and the moon. Every rocket fired from the Kennedy Space Center is tracked electronically to determine if it is on course through the use of maps made by surveyors. The technological complexity of such undertakings allows surveyors to delegate more tasks than ever to technicians.

THE JOB

As essential assistants to civil engineers, surveyors, and mapmakers, surveying and mapping technicians are usually the first to be involved in any job that requires precise plotting. This includes highways, airports, housing developments, mines, dams, bridges, and buildings of all kinds.

The surveying and mapping technician is a key worker in field parties and major surveying projects and is often assigned the position of chief instrument worker under the surveyor's supervision. Technicians use a variety of surveying instruments, including the theodolite, transit, level, and other electronic equipment, to measure distances or locate a position. Technicians may be *rod workers,* using level rods or range poles to make elevation and distance measurements. They may also be *chain workers,* measuring shorter distances using a surveying chain or a metal tape. During the survey, it is important to accurately record all readings and keep orderly field notes to check for accuracy.

Surveying and mapping technicians may specialize if they join a firm that focuses on one or more particular types of surveying. In a firm that specializes in land surveying, technicians are highly skilled in technical measuring and tasks related to establishing township, property, and other tract-of-land boundary lines. They help the professional surveyor with maps, notes, and title deeds. They help survey the land, check the accuracy of existing records, and prepare legal documents such as deeds and leases.

Similarly, technicians who work for highway, pipeline, railway, or power line surveying firms help to establish grades, lines, and other points of reference for construction projects. This survey information provides the exact locations for engineering design and construction work.

Technicians who work for geodetic surveyors help take measurements of large masses of land, sea, or space. These measurements must take into account the curvature of the earth and its geophysical characteristics. Their findings set major points of reference for smaller land surveys, determining national boundaries, and preparing maps.

Technicians may also specialize in hydrographic surveying, measuring harbors, rivers, and other bodies of water. These surveys are needed to design navigation systems, prepare nautical maps and charts, establish property boundaries, and plan for breakwaters, levees, dams, locks, piers, and bridges.

Mining surveying technicians are usually on the geological staffs of either mining companies or exploration companies. In recent years, costly new surveying instruments have changed the way they do their jobs. Using highly technical machinery, technicians can map underground geology, take samples, locate diamond drill holes, log drill cores, and map geological data derived from boreholes. They also map data on mine plans and diagrams and help the geologist determine ore reserves. In the search for new mines, technicians operate delicate instruments to obtain data on variations in the earth's magnetic field, its conductivity, and gravity. They use their data to map the boundaries of areas for potential further exploration.

Surveying and mapping technicians may find topographical surveys to be interesting and challenging work. These surveys determine the contours of the land and indicate such features as mountains, lakes, rivers, forests, roads, farms, buildings, and other distinguishable landmarks. In topographical surveying, technicians help take aerial or land photographs with photogrammetric equipment installed in an airplane or ground station that can take pictures of large areas. This method is widely used to measure farmland planted with certain crops and to verify crop average allotments under government production planning quotas.

A large number of survey technicians are employed in construction work. Technicians are needed from start to finish on any job. They check the construction of a structure for size, height, depth, level, and form specifications. They also use measurements to locate the critical construction points as specified by design plans, such as corners of buildings, foundation points, center points for columns, walls, and other features, floor or ceiling levels, and other features that require precise measurements and location.

Technological advances such as the Global Positioning System (GPS) and geographic information systems (GIS) have revolutionized surveying and mapping work. Using these systems, surveying teams can track points on the earth with radio signals transmitted from satellites and store this information in computer databases.

REQUIREMENTS

High School

If you are interested in becoming a surveying and mapping technician, take mathematics courses, such as algebra, geometry, and trigonometry, as well as mechanical drawing in high school. Physics, chemistry, and biology are other valuable classes that will help you gain laboratory experience. Reading, writing, and comprehension skills as well as knowledge of computers are also vital in surveying and mapping, so English and computer science courses are also highly recommended.

Postsecondary Training

Though not required to enter the field, graduates of accredited postsecondary training programs for surveying, photogrammetry, and mapping are in the best position to become surveying and mapping technicians. Postsecondary training is available from institutional programs and correspondence schools. These demanding technical programs generally last two years with a possible field study in the summer. First-year courses include English, composition, drafting, applied mathematics, surveying and measurements, construction materials and methods, applied physics, statistics, and computer applications. Second-year courses cover subjects such as technical physics, advanced surveying, photogrammetry and mapping, soils and foundations, technical reporting, legal issues, and transportation and environmental engineering. Contact the American Congress on Surveying and Mapping (ACSM) for a list of accredited programs (see the end of this article for contact information).

With additional experience and study, technicians can specialize in geodesy, topography, hydrography, or photogrammetry. Many graduates of two-year programs later pursue a bachelor's degree in surveying, engineering, or geomatics.

Certification or Licensing

Unlike professional land surveyors, there are no certification or licensing requirements for becoming a surveying and mapping technician. However, technicians who seek government employment must pass a civil service examination.

Many employers prefer certified technicians for promotions into higher positions with more responsibility. The National Society of Professional Surveyors, a member organization of the ACSM, offers the voluntary survey technician certification at four levels. With each level, the technician must have more experience and pass progressively challenging examinations. If the technician hopes one day to work as a surveyor, he or she must be specially certified to work in his or her state.

Other Requirements

To be a successful surveying and mapping technician, you must be patient, orderly, systematic, accurate, and objective in your work. You must be willing to work cooperatively and have the ability to think and plan ahead. Because of the increasing technical nature of their work, you must have computer skills to be able to use highly complex equipment such as GPS and GIS technology.

EXPLORING

One of the best opportunities for experience is to work part time or during your summer vacation for a construction firm or a company involved in survey work. Even if the job does not involve direct contact with survey crews, you may be able to observe their work and converse with them to discover more about their daily activities. Another possibility is to work for a government agency overseeing land use. The Bureau of Land Management, for example, has employment opportunities for students who qualify, as well as many volunteer positions. The Forest Service also offers temporary positions for students.

EMPLOYERS

There are approximately 65,000 surveying and mapping technicians working in the United States. Almost two-thirds of technicians find work with engineering or architectural service firms. The federal government also employs a number of technicians to work for the U.S. Geological Survey, the Bureau of Land Management, the National Oceanic and Atmospheric Administration, the National Imagery and Mapping Agency, and the Forest Service. State and local governments also hire surveying and mapping technicians to work for highway departments and urban planning agencies. Construction firms and oil, gas, and mining companies also hire technicians.

STARTING OUT

If you plan on entering surveying straight from high school, you may first work as an apprentice. Through on-the-job training and some classroom work, apprentices build up their skills and knowledge of the trade to eventually become surveying and mapping technicians.

If you plan to attend a technical institute or four-year college, contact your school's career services office for help in arranging examinations or interviews. Employers of surveying technicians often send recruiters to schools before graduation and arrange to employ promising graduates. Some community or technical colleges have work-study programs that provide cooperative part-time or summer work for pay. Employers involved with these programs often hire students full time after graduation.

Finally, many cities have employment agencies that specialize in placing technical workers in positions in surveying, mapping, construction, mining, and related fields. Check your local newspaper, telephone book, or surf the Web to see if your town offers these services.

ADVANCEMENT

Possibilities for advancement are linked to levels of formal education and experience. As technicians gain experience and technical knowledge, they can advance to positions of greater responsibility and eventually work as chief surveyor. To advance into this position, technicians will most likely need a two- or four-year degree in surveying and many years of experience. Also, all 50 states require surveyors to be licensed, requiring varying amounts of experience, education, and examinations.

Regardless of the level of advancement, all surveying and mapping technicians must continue studying to keep up with the technological developments in their field. Technological advances in computers, lasers, and microcomputers will continue to change job requirements. Studying to keep up with changes combined with progressive experience gained on the job will increase the technician's opportunity for advancement.

EARNINGS

According to the U.S. Department of Labor, the 2005 median hourly salary for all surveying and mapping technicians, regardless of the industry, was $15.04 (amounting to $31,290 for full-time work). The lowest paid 10 percent earned less than $9.28 ($19,300 for full-time work), and the highest paid 10 percent earned over $25.00 an hour (or $52,000 annually for full-time work). Technicians working for the public sector in federal, state, and local governments generally earn more per hour than those working in the private sector for engineering and architectural services. In 2005, surveying and mapping technicians working for the federal government made a mean salary of $41,720 per year.

WORK ENVIRONMENT

Surveying and mapping technicians usually work about 40 hours a week except when overtime is necessary. The peak work period for many kinds of surveying work is during the summer months when weather conditions are most favorable. However, surveying crews are exposed to all types of weather conditions.

Some survey projects involve certain hazards depending upon the region and the climate as well as local plant and animal life. Field survey crews may encounter snakes and poison ivy. They are subject to heat exhaustion, sunburn, and frostbite. Some projects, particularly those being conducted near construction projects or busy highways, impose dangers of injury from cars and flying debris. Unless survey technicians are employed for office assignments, their work location changes from survey to survey. Some assignments may require technicians to be away from home for varying periods of time.

While on the job, technicians who supervise other workers must take special care to observe good safety practices. Construction and mining workplaces usually require hard hats, special clothing, and protective shoes.

OUTLOOK

Employment for surveying and mapping technicians is expected to grow about as fast as the average for all occupations through 2014, according to the U.S. Department of Labor. New technologies— such as GPS, GIS, and remote sensing—have increased the accuracy and productivity of professionals in the field, which may reduce employment growth.

One factor that may increase the demand for surveying services, and therefore surveying technicians, is growth in urban and suburban areas. New streets, homes, shopping centers, schools, and gas and water lines will require property and boundary line surveys. Other factors are the continuing state and federal highway improvement programs and the increasing number of urban redevelopment programs. The expansion of industrial and business firms and the relocation of some firms in large undeveloped areas are also expected to create a need for surveying services.

The need to replace workers who have either retired or transferred to other occupations will also provide opportunities. In general, technicians with more education and skill training will have more job options.

FOR MORE INFORMATION

For more information on accredited surveying programs, contact
Accreditation Board for Engineering and Technology
111 Market Place, Suite 1050
Baltimore, MD 21202-4012
Tel: 410-347-7700
http://www.abet.org

For information on careers, scholarships, certification, and educational programs, contact
American Congress on Surveying and Mapping
Six Montgomery Village Avenue, Suite 403
Gaithersburg, MD 20879-3557

Tel: 240-632-9716
Email: lee.canfield@acsm.net
http://www.acsm.net

For information about the Bureau of Land Management and its responsibilities, visit its Web site.
Bureau of Land Management
Office of Public Affairs
1849 C Street, Room 406-LS
Washington, DC 20240-0001
Tel: 202-452-5125
http://www.blm.gov

For information on certification, contact
National Society of Professional Surveyors
Six Montgomery Village Avenue, Suite 403
Gaithersburg, MD 20879-3557
Tel: 240-632-9716
http://www.nspsmo.org

For more information on Geographic Information Systems (GIS), visit the following Web site:
GIS.com
http://www.gis.com

Surveyors

OVERVIEW

Surveyors mark exact measurements and locations of elevations, points, lines, and contours on or near the earth's surface. They measure distances between points to determine property boundaries and to provide data for mapmaking, construction projects, and other engineering purposes. There are approximately 131,000 surveyors, cartographers, photogrammetrists, and surveying technicians employed in the United States. Of those, about 56,000 are surveyors and about 11,000 are cartographers and photogrammetrists.

HISTORY

As the United States expanded from the Atlantic to the Pacific, people moved over the mountains and plains into the uncharted regions of the West. They found it necessary to chart their routes and to mark property lines and borderlines by surveying and filing claims.

The need for accurate geographical measurements and precise records of those measurements has increased over the years. Surveying measurements are needed to determine the location of a trail, highway, or road; the site of a log cabin, frame house, or skyscraper; the right-of-way for water pipes, drainage ditches, and telephone lines; and for the charting of unexplored regions, bodies of water, land, and underground mines.

As a result, the demand for professional surveyors has grown and become more complex. New computerized systems are now used to map, store, and retrieve geographical data more accurately and efficiently. This new technology has not only improved the process

School Subjects
Geography
Mathematics

Personal Skills
Communication/ideas
Technical/scientific

Work Environment
Primarily outdoors
Primarily multiple locations

Minimum Education Level
Some postsecondary training

Salary Range
$25,530 to $45,860 to
$75,870+

Certification or Licensing
Required

Outlook
About as fast as the average

DOT
018

GOE
02.08.01

NOC
2154

O*NET-SOC
17-1022.00

of surveying but extended its reach as well. Surveyors can now make detailed maps of ocean floors and the moon's surface.

THE JOB

On proposed construction projects, such as highways, airstrips, and housing developments, it is the surveyor's responsibility to make necessary measurements through an accurate and detailed survey of the area. The surveyor usually works with a field party consisting of several people. Instrument assistants, called *surveying and mapping technicians*, handle a variety of surveying instruments including the theodolite, transit, level, surveyor's chain, rod, and other electronic equipment. In the course of the survey, it is important that all readings be recorded accurately and field notes maintained so that the survey can be checked for accuracy.

Surveyors may specialize in one or more particular types of surveying.

Land surveyors establish township, property, and other tract-of-land boundary lines. Using maps, notes, or actual land title deeds, they survey the land, checking for the accuracy of existing records. This information is used to prepare legal documents such as deeds and leases. *Land surveying managers* coordinate the work of surveyors, their parties, and legal, engineering, architectural, and other staff involved in a project. In addition, these managers develop policy, prepare budgets, certify work upon completion, and handle numerous other administrative duties.

Highway surveyors establish grades, lines, and other points of reference for highway construction projects. This survey information is essential to the work of the numerous engineers and the construction crews who build the new highway.

Geodetic surveyors measure large masses of land, sea, and space that must take into account the curvature of the earth and its geophysical characteristics. Their work is helpful in establishing points of reference for smaller land surveys, determining national boundaries, and preparing maps. Geodetic computers calculate latitude, longitude, angles, areas, and other information needed for mapmaking. They work from field notes made by an engineering survey party and also use reference tables and a calculating machine or computer.

Marine surveyors measure harbors, rivers, and other bodies of water. They determine the depth of the water through measuring sound waves in relation to nearby landmasses. Their work is essential for planning and constructing navigation projects, such as breakwaters, dams, piers, marinas, and bridges, and for preparing nautical charts and maps.

A surveyor uses a laser transit at a job site. *(David R. Frazier/The Image Works)*

Mine surveyors make surface and underground surveys, preparing maps of mines and mining operations. Such maps are helpful in examining underground passages within the levels of a mine and assessing the volume and location of raw material available.

Geophysical prospecting surveyors locate and mark sites considered likely to contain petroleum deposits. *Oil-well directional surveyors* use sonic, electronic, and nuclear measuring instruments to gauge the presence and amount of oil- and gas-bearing reservoirs. *Pipeline surveyors* determine rights-of-way for oil construction projects, providing information essential to the preparation for and laying of the lines.

Photogrammetric engineers determine the contour of an area to show elevations and depressions and indicate such features as mountains, lakes, rivers, forests, roads, farms, buildings, and other landmarks. Aerial, land, and water photographs are taken with special equipment able to capture images of very large areas. From these pictures, accurate measurements of the terrain and surface features can be made. These surveys are helpful in construction projects and in the preparation of topographical maps. Photogrammetry is particularly helpful in charting areas that are inaccessible or difficult to travel.

REQUIREMENTS

High School

Does this work interest you? If so, you should prepare for it by taking plenty of math and science courses in high school. Take algebra, geometry, and trigonometry to become comfortable making different calculations. Earth science, chemistry, and physics classes should also be helpful. Geography will help you learn about different locations, their characteristics, and cartography. Benefits from taking mechanical drawing and other drafting classes include an increased ability to visualize abstractions, exposure to detailed work, and an understanding of perspectives. Taking computer science classes will prepare you for working with technical surveying equipment.

Postsecondary Training

Depending on state requirements, you will need some postsecondary education. The quickest route is by earning a bachelor's degree in surveying or engineering combined with on-the-job training. Other entry options include obtaining more job experience combined with a one- to three-year program in surveying and surveying technology offered by community colleges, technical institutes, and vocational schools.

Certification or Licensing

All 50 states require that surveyors making property and boundary surveys be licensed or registered. The requirements for licensure vary, but most require a degree in surveying or a related field, a certain number of years of experience, and passing examinations in land surveying. Generally, the higher the degree obtained, the less experience required. Those with bachelor's degrees may need only two to four years of on-the-job experience, while those with a lesser degree may need up to 12 years of prior experience to obtain a license. Information on specific requirements can be obtained by contacting the licensure department of the state in which you plan to work. If you are seeking employment in the federal government, you must take a civil service examination and meet the educational, experience, and other specified requirements for the position.

Other Requirements

The ability to work with numbers and perform mathematical computations accurately and quickly is very important. Other helpful qualities are the ability to visualize and understand objects in two and three dimensions (spatial relationships) and the ability to discriminate between and compare shapes, sizes, lines, shadings, and other forms (form perception).

Surveyors walk a great deal and carry equipment over all types of terrain so endurance and coordination are important physical assets. In addition, surveyors direct and supervise the work of their team, so you should be good at working with other people and demonstrate leadership abilities.

EXPLORING

While you are in high school, begin to familiarize yourself with terms, projects, and tools used in this profession by reading books and magazines on the topic. One magazine that is available online is *Professional Surveyor Magazine* at http://www.profsurv.com. One of the best opportunities for experience is a summer job with a construction outfit or company that requires survey work. Even if the job does not involve direct contact with survey crews, it will offer an opportunity to observe surveyors and talk with them about their work.

Some colleges have work-study programs that offer on-the-job experience. These opportunities, like summer or part-time jobs, provide helpful contacts in the field that may lead to future full-time employment. If your college does not offer a work-study program and you can't find a paying summer job, consider volunteering at an appropriate government agency. The U.S. Geological Survey and the Bureau of Land Management usually have volunteer opportunities in select areas.

EMPLOYERS

According to the U.S. Department of Labor, almost two-thirds of surveying workers in the United States are employed in engineering, architectural, and surveying firms. Federal, state, and local government agencies are the next largest employers of surveying workers, and the majority of the remaining surveyors work for construction firms, oil and gas extraction companies, and public utilities. Only a small number of surveyors are self-employed.

STARTING OUT

Apprentices with a high school education can enter the field as equipment operators or surveying assistants. Those who have postsecondary education can enter the field more easily, beginning as surveying and mapping technicians.

College graduates can learn about job openings through their schools' career services offices or through potential employers that may visit their campus. Many cities have employment agencies that specialize in seeking out workers for positions in surveying and related fields. Check your local newspaper or telephone book to see if such recruiting firms exist in your area.

ADVANCEMENT

With experience, workers advance through the leadership ranks within a surveying team. Workers begin as assistants and then can move into positions such as senior technician, party chief, and, finally, licensed surveyor. Because surveying work is closely related to other fields, surveyors can move into electrical, mechanical, or chemical engineering or specialize in drafting.

EARNINGS

In 2005, surveyors earned a median annual salary of $45,860, according to the U.S. Department of Labor. The middle 50 percent earned between $33,960 and $60,730 a year. The lowest paid 10 percent earned less than $25,530, and the highest paid 10 percent earned more than $75,870 a year. In general, the federal government paid the highest wages to its surveyors, $66,710 a year in 2005.

Most positions with the federal, state, and local governments and with private firms provide life and medical insurance, pension, vacation, and holiday benefits.

WORK ENVIRONMENT

Surveyors work 40-hour weeks except when overtime is necessary to meet a project deadline. The peak work period is during the summer months when weather conditions are most favorable. However, it is not uncommon for the surveyor to be exposed to adverse weather conditions.

Some survey projects may involve hazardous conditions, depending on the region and climate as well as the plant and animal life. Survey crews may encounter snakes, poison ivy, and other hazardous plant and animal life, and may suffer heat exhaustion, sunburn, and frostbite while in the field. Survey projects, particularly those near construction projects or busy highways, may impose dangers of injury from heavy traffic, flying objects, and other accidental hazards. Unless the surveyor is employed only for office assignments, the work location most likely will change from survey to survey. Some assignments may require the surveyor to be away from home for periods of time.

OUTLOOK

The U.S. Department of Labor predicts the employment of surveyors will grow about as fast as the average for all occupations through 2014. The outlook is best for surveyors who have college degrees and advanced field experience. Despite slower growth, the widespread use of technology, such as the Global Positioning System and geographic information systems, will provide jobs to surveyors with strong technical and computer skills.

Growth in urban and suburban areas (with the need for new streets, homes, shopping centers, schools, gas and water lines) will provide employment opportunities. State and federal highway improvement programs and local urban redevelopment programs also will provide jobs for surveyors. The expansion of industrial and business firms and the relocation of some firms to large undeveloped tracts will also create job openings. However, construction projects are closely tied to the state of the economy, so employment may fluctuate from year to year.

FOR MORE INFORMATION

For information on state affiliates and colleges and universities offering land surveying programs, contact
American Congress on Surveying and Mapping
Six Montgomery Village Avenue, Suite 403
Gaithersburg, MD 20879-3557
Tel: 240-632-9716
Email: lee.canfield@acsm.net
http://www.acsm.net

For information on awards and recommended books to read, contact or check out the following Web sites:

American Association for Geodetic Surveying
Six Montgomery Village Avenue, Suite 403
Gaithersburg, MD 20879-3557
Tel: 240-632-9716
Email: aagsmo@acsm.net
http://www.aagsmo.org

National Society of Professional Surveyors
Six Montgomery Village Avenue, Suite 403
Gaithersburg, MD 20879-3557
Tel: 240-632-9716
http://www.nspsmo.org

For information on photogrammetry and careers in the field, contact
American Society for Photogrammetry and Remote Sensing
5410 Grosvenor Lane, Suite 210
Bethesda, MD 20814-2160
Tel: 301-493-0290
Email: asprs@asprs.org
http://www.asprs.org

For information on volunteer opportunities with the federal government, contact
Bureau of Land Management
Office of Public Affairs
1849 C Street, Room 406-LS
Washington, DC 20240-0001
Tel: 202-452-5125
http://www.blm.gov

U.S. Geological Survey
12201 Sunrise Valley Drive
Reston, VA 20192-0002
Tel: 888-275-8747
http://www.usgs.gov

Index

Entries and page numbers in **bold** indicate major treatment of a topic.

WITHDRAWAL